RELIEF & DEVELOPMENT

SOCIAL JUSTICE

DISCIPLESHIP

MEDICINE

# WHEN EVERYTHING IS MISSIONS

CLEAN WATER

EVANGELISM

BY DENNY SPITTERS
& MATTHEW ELLISON

ORPHAN CARE

CHURCH PLANTING

*When Everything Is Missions*
by Denny Spitters & Matthew Ellison

copyright ©2017 Pioneers-USA & Sixteen:Fifteen
ISBN: 9780989954549

This book was published by BottomLine Media, an imprint of Pioneers, that celebrates the "bottom line" of God's covenant with Abraham: "I will bless all nations through you." To purchase other BottomLine titles, visit *Pioneers.org/Store.* This book is available in ebook format on Apple iBooks and Amazon Kindle.

# PRAISE FOR *WHEN EVERYTHING IS MISSIONS*

"Pastors, mission committees, mission agencies, and church leaders would do well to read the new (and short!) book, *When Everything Is Mission*. ... Spitters and Ellison remind us that if we think all of this is missions we will end up neglecting the very task laid out for us in the Great Commission. When everything is missions, missions gets left behind."

> — *Kevin DeYoung, Senior Pastor, Christ Covenant Church,*
> *Mathews, North Carolina*

"This brief, powerful and provocative book should be read by every North American pastor. Spitters and Ellison contend that when every Christian is a missionary and every ministry is missions, we gut the mandate to reach all nations. Check it out to discover why they think such is the case."

> — *J. D. Payne, Pastor for Church Multiplication, The Church at*
> *Brook Hills, Birmingham, Alabama*

"I welcome the publication of this book. Among many other insightful contributions, Denny and Matthew get the important distinction between a popular understanding of "missionary" and the technical understanding of "missionary." They rightly insist that we don't obscure the technical understanding and argue biblically for the importance of maintaining it. May this book be used to recruit, train and mobilize God's people toward crossing cultures to bring the love and justice of Jesus to the unreached and unengaged peoples of the world."

> — *Tom Steller, Pastor for Leadership Development,*
> *Bethlehem Baptist Church; Assoc. Professor of New Testament;*
> *Senior Advisor; Dean of Global and Alumni Outreach,*
> *Bethlehem College and Seminary, Minneapolis, Minnesota*

"It's difficult to fathom that a practice as essential and traditional to the church through the millenia as 'missions' would require a fresh update. Yet, that is is exactly what is needed today and just what Denny Spitters and Matthew Ellison set out to do. Through a series of seven critical questions, the authors will challenge how you think about, and more importantly, what you do about taking the good news of Jesus to those who have never heard. This book is both theologically deep and practically wide. It's a must read for preaching pastors who long for clarity in exhorting the local church to live on mission with Jesus."

*—Dave Bruskas, Lead Pastor, North Church*
*Albuquerque, New Mexico*

"Denny Spitters and Matthew Ellison have done the churches of the new millennium a great service. *When Everything Is Missions* is just the book for churches struggling with how to envision and fulfill their part in God's global purposes in the world. In it they will find that fine balance of the theoretical and conceptual based on a rock-solid understanding of the Scriptures, combined with practical and proven steps that any church can take to get in the game and do its part in the Great Task. I recommend it highly."

*— Gary Corwin, Missiologist with SIM International and*
*Associate Editor of Evangelical Missions Quarterly*

"For far too long many churches have become either distracted or sidelined by prevailing misconceptions of what their mission to the world should be. Thankfully through this book, Spitters and Ellison have taken up the banner of giving much needed correction to misunderstandings and mistaken mission practices that have become prevalent in many church mission programs. Tactfully yet candidly, the authors tackle these issues in a clear and helpful manner."

*— Marvin Newell, Senior Vice-President of Missio Nexus*

"One of my mentors frequently reminds me, 'Where there's a mist in the pulpit, there's a fog in the pew.' Nowhere are these words more applicable than in relation to the mission of the Church. The health and impact of the Church has always correlated to the clarity of her mission. Who has God called us to be, and what has he commanded us to do? In a time of growing confusion, particularly in the West, about the nature of missions and the role of missionaries, Denny Spitters and Matthew Ellison turn on the fog lamps. This book will sharpen your perspective, as a church or mission leader, with regard to one of the watershed issues of our time."

*— Steve Richardson, President of Pioneers-USA*

"The first years of the 21st century have seen more than 300 movements, mostly in the global South. Many of these movements represent an engagement with unreached or unengaged people groups of urban social segments. All of these movements are shaped by kingdom values and lifestyles, as well as a clear kingdom-of-God vision regarding finishing the task. At the same time, one of the serious challenges of the global North church over the last decades is sometimes called mission drift. In *When Everything is Missions,* Denny Spitters, and Matthew Ellison take on several critical "drift" issues. To this task they bring both biblical clarity and a passionate call for kingdom-minded churches to embrace the sacrifices required to make disciples and plant churches everywhere people are living and dying without a viable Jesus option."

*— Jerry Trousdale, Director of International Ministries, Cityteam International; author of* Miraculous Movements: How Hundreds of Thousands of Muslims are Falling in Love with Jesus

"When we love deeply, it requires we think deeply. Denny and Matthew's love for the nations compels them to think deeply about what this means. This book will lead you into a conversation about missions. God's love for the nations demands our lives, our soul, our all. Grab this book to engage your heart and mind in deeper engagement among the nations."

*— Pastor Phil Auxier, Crestview Bible Church Hutchinson, Kansas*

"The truth can sting. In an age where you can go far and wide in the Church and never hear about the Great Commission, this book gives a good hurt, and a needed one. Exhortations and solutions to first-world problems are fine, but they are not the full story. Hopefully, this book will penetrate both pulpit and pew to provide a catalyst for world-rocking change. Read it and weep over our selfishness, then get going."

*— Pastor Chip Lusko, Calvary Chapel*

"As Matthew and Denny clearly demonstrate, the Western portion of God's earthly body has been infected with cultural values that downplay clear definitions and dilute distinctions that God has created to reflect His glory among the nations. Although the Spirit-guided examination, diagnosis, and strong medicine they recommend will be painful for many individuals and churches to hear and receive, *When Everything Is Missions* is precisely what the Great Physician knows His people need to fulfill His mission."

*— Pastor Jeff Jackson,*
*Shepherd's Staff Mission Facilitators*

"In over forty years in local church ministry I have seen a growing number of churches focusing more on methodology of missions rather than the biblical foundation of missions. The result has been a diluted global ministry. *When Everything Is Missions* pinpoints the critical issues that need to be evaluated. It is very practical, providing questions for continued dialogue and evaluation. Here is a call to reaffirm foundational truths and practices. I highly recommend this book as an important tool for a local church to have an effective global impact."

*— Steve Beirn, author of* Well Sent: Reimagining the Church's Missionary-Sending Process; *Global Ministries Pastor Calvary Church, Lancaster, PA*

# CONTENTS

*If everything is mission, nothing is mission.*
*If everything the church does is to be classed as*
*"mission," we shall need to find another term...* [1]

— Stephen Neill


*It would seem more biblical to say, 'If everything*
*is mission... everything is mission.'...*
*[E]verything a Christian and a Christian church*
*is, says, and does should be missional in its*
*conscious participation in the mission of God in*
*God's world.* [2]

— Christopher Wright

# FOREWORD

AS A TEACHER, every semester for the last 21 years I have asked college students, "What is the kingdom of God?" More than 90 percent of the students reference a place (heaven). Though the kingdom of God is arguably the central teaching of Jesus (see Acts 1:3) as well as Paul (see Acts 28:30-31), most Christian students have no clue what the words mean. That doesn't stop them from using this term on a regular basis as if they know *exactly* what it means.

I've also asked thousands of students for a biblical definition of a *disciple* or *discipleship*. Usually they answer with a contemporary definition of the day, never referring to Christ's descriptions of a disciple. My own denomination went down such a road in the 1980s with a series of workbooks and an hour on Sunday evenings called Discipleship Training which made everyone who attended believe they were being discipled even though the program lacked much resemblance to biblical discipleship.

In 40 years of ministry I've been amazed at how casual the Christian community can be in using biblical terms that are rarely fully defined or only superficially defined through the Christian cultural trends of the day. In addition, many of us may tend to accept and parrot ideas and definitions we hear from a stage on Sunday mornings without much critical thought.

Yet how we define words matters. In the Christian community, defining words give direction to our faith and practice; words shape our understanding of the ultimate purposes of God to which our communities of faith are dedicated. Good definitions energize our efforts and call us to unity.

I am passionate about teaching and love to see my students integrate discipleship seamlessly into every area of their lives. Encouraging them to disregard or do away with definitions, however, does them a great disservice.

I teach a class on the global context of the Christian faith. When we finish the semester I ask my students if they believe that every Christian is a missionary and 99 percent say yes. Then I ask them if they think I believe that everyone is a missionary. The same 99 percent say yes. They are shocked when I say I don't believe that everyone is a missionary. I do believe that every follower of Christ is to live strategic intentional lives engaged in God's global purpose both locally and internationally every day. Does that make them missionaries? I would say it's not the same thing.

**May our mission definitions be driven not by our personal interests, prejudices, and preferences, but by the passions and purpose of the God of all nations.**

Denny Spitters and Matthew Ellison tackle these very questions. What do the terms missions and missionary mean? What do we mean when we use them? Is everything we do missions? Is every Christian essentially a missionary?

As you wrestle with the questions Denny and Matthew raise, my prayer is that you will do so with an open and critical mind as well as a gracious, understanding heart. May this book spur you on! Every generation needs voices that will challenge contemporary trends that seem to be rooted in a weak or shallow approach to understanding Scripture and history. We need to be alert to our human tendency to adopt seemingly new concepts, support them with proof texts, bolster them with weak arguments, and then find someone in the church to champion the idea and integrate these concepts into our existing culture and programs, thinking we are moving ahead.

In such a way, far too many churches and believers have justified pursuing only their personal passions disconnected from the global context of the mission of God and His ordained methods for accomplishing His purposes. This is just what happened in far too many of the churches that embraced "missional" language as it came in vogue without participating in the rigorous exercise of examining the Scriptures for direction on engaging with the mission of God.

The task of definition is not one that should be accomplished in isolation or by only the present Christian generation. Many have gone before us; we can rejoice that we have a great cloud of witnesses. Any attempt to define our mission requires a careful study of biblical languages and an accurate understanding of biblical context, history, and the trajectory of the apostolic faith.

This book tackles a core issue that relates to the very DNA of the Church. It calls us to rediscover and embrace the central plot of the story of God, His Church, and her role in God's mission. May our mission definitions be driven not by our personal interests, prejudices, and preferences, but by the passions and purpose of the God of all nations. My prayer, my deep hope, is that this book will be catalyst for critical thought and conversation, solid biblical exegesis, and faithful application in the Church.

*— Jeff Lewis*
*Director of Mobilization*
*California Baptist University*

# INTRODUCTION

THE 7 P.M. MEETING at First Christian Church seemed to race; it seemed as if only 30 minutes had passed. John looked up at the digits: 8:37. His stomach was churning. Why was this so difficult for him?

As Executive and Missions Pastor he knew the facts. The church had a $150,000 budget deficit. The missions fund contained $200,000. They would need to balance the budget now and cut the support of five missions workers who, for all the time and money they cost, had shown poor results or return on investment.

John's training and background had made him adept at reading a profit-and-loss report. He got it. Board Chairman Jim Taylor's curt statement and Pastor Steve's approving nod made things quite clear; these cuts had to happen.

Still, a battery of conflicting emotions, Bible verses, books he had read, and personal convictions he wasn't quite sure about made him unsteady, unsure of what it was he even believed about missions after five years in his role. Meetings like this sucked the life out of John not just because they meant making tough decisions but also because they left him with the distinct impression that nobody, including himself, really even understood what missions at FCC was all about.

He was especially uneasy with the fervor of those who stated, "Every ministry in our church is a missions ministry; our church is a mission. We are a missional church."

On the surface it sounded great, and he had embraced these concepts for the past seven years since Pastor Steve had become their new pastor. Yet, frankly, as John thought about the ardor behind the "everybody is a missionary" concept, and the metamorphosis of FCC into a "missional" church, the mantra seemed to over-promise and under-deliver. He couldn't shake this thought. It made his stomach ache a little more.

**John, I see no difference whatsoever between sharing the gospel here or somewhere else.**

As John offered a mild protest against using the missions fund to cover the deficit, one board member had blurted out, "John, I see no difference whatsoever between sharing the gospel here or somewhere else. Sharing the gospel is missions. Missions is doing evangelism. Doesn't Acts 1:8 mention Jerusalem as well as the ends of the earth? What's the difference? We have people at home, right here, all around us who are unreached—this is our mission field and everything our church does IS missions!"

Any protests to that seemed hollow. This is our mission field and everything is missions, period.

As Missions Pastor, John was leading missions mostly by creating more programs and activity. He had bypassed the time, energy, and effort of any process that would define a compelling, biblical, definition of missions for FCC, and this meeting was a reflection of that. Maybe the cart was in front of the horse.

The next morning John woke up thinking about FCC, its history, and its history in missions, as well as his own history at the church; maybe these would shed some light on what happened at the meeting.

John was a favorite son at FCC. His parents, married there in 1969, still attended. He grew up at FCC and had a lot of his life invested in his church. He married Jo there in 1995.

Since it began in 1956, First Christian Church had been known as a missions-minded church. Ten local families joined with a bi-vocational pastor to plant the church during the post-war baby boom. Immediately they started supporting a missionary family in Peru. By 1970 FCC was a church of 400 that embraced sharing the gospel by sending missionaries overseas. "Missions" meant saving foreigners overseas.

Due to its premier location in a fast-growing suburb, FCC become a well-known mega-church of 2,000 by 1985. John was only 12 at the time but well remembered the annual mission conferences of those years, headlined by strange visitors from countries he had never heard of. As giving increased, the mission budget grew to support more than 20 families, couples, or individual missionaries. The belief was that more money meant more missionaries and more missionaries meant more missions.

But by 2006, with 4,000 attendees and a missions budget of $1 million to support some 70 workers, FCC was having issues that would change its future dramatically.

Discipleship at FCC meant becoming a member; evangelism and outreach meant giving a sacrificial faith pledge to missions. Few could remember anyone new coming to Christ through the influence of church members during the last decade. Transfer growth and a great preaching pastor had sustained them.

The last five years had been stagnant, though, and the 2007 economic downturn brought on the deficit that required such cuts now. To complicate matters, a youth leader had been let go for improper use of church funds, leading a growing group of families to depart for other churches with better programs for their kids. Attendance was slowly spiraling down.

The year 2007 was also when the pastor of 25 years retired and church leaders began looking for a new pastor who could stem the tide.

They found their answer in 32-year-old Steve Cates. A passionate communicator, he outlined a vibrant vision for a "missional" church where discipleship and missions meant "being on mission with God in your own context." In 2010 Pastor Steve recruited John to oversee the staff as Executive Pastor, and after a year John took on the role of Missions Pastor as well.

When he came on board John found FCC more fragmented than he had realized. He was aware of some of the strife and disunity that had developed between the pastor, church leaders, and church body, especially in the area of "missions." Pastor Steve had told him as much. Missions "faith pledges" were down and notices were sent to 20 foreign workers communicating that they were on the bubble for a support reduction or termination unless they could show more significant, missional results.

John shifted more and more missions funding toward "native missionaries" who could do mission work for less than sending an American family overseas. The security, cost, and training issues made hiring indigenous national workers a great return on investment.

Pastor Steve was getting frustrated with the church's lack of response to his missional paradigm. His desire to turn FCC into a disciple-making church where people shared the gospel within their work, school, and neighborhood context was stalled if not suspended. He believed that if the congregation would embrace living, working, and thinking as missionaries, results would follow. They hadn't.

Pastor Steve believed that all missions and evangelism activity fit into concentric circles. Serving at home, first and foremost (your "Jerusalem," in Acts 1:8 terms), was the key to mission. He had decided long ago that most of the talk about missions was semantics; sharing the gospel was all that was important, and it didn't matter where. When he talked about outreach, he regularly said, "Missions is the mission of the church!" With all of the "lost" in their city, shouldn't evangelism be the main focus and mission of the church—the central reason for its existence? Aren't evangelism and missions essentially one?

• • •

This story may describe the reality for some of our churches. Church leaders may be uncertain if they should fight to protect old paradigms and programs or jettison them as deadweight in a new and changing world. Many churches find themselves at a loss to define their global mission. Others have become so ingrown with all of the problems of existence, survival, and relevance that their mission efforts are all about their church. Shared language may not indicate shared understanding, with clear definitions of discipleship, evangelism, outreach, missions, missionaries, missional, and mission of God rarely found, even or maybe especially in churches that proclaim all of us are missionaries and all our ministries are mission.

> **Many churches find themselves at a loss to define their global mission.**

One of the obstacles is that processes like building consensus, hammering out definitions, and developing policies that reflect a shared understanding can be slow, painful work. If we place a higher value on getting things done, we may prefer to spend our time and energy responding to missionary needs and funding requests as they come rather than taking the time to invest in a process of biblical discovery that might lead to a coherent and compelling understanding of our mission which could guide all those decisions and activities.

We contend that many churches do not do missions well because they don't think about missions well. As a result, many North American churches miss much of their opportunity to be part of the global plans God has for His whole Church.

If words have meaning, then their definitions and uses matter. When everything is missions, some of the most central aspects may be lost or buried—such as sending our own to make disciples and plant churches cross-culturally. An over-emphasis on getting bang for our buck may also lead us to ministries that make us feel good or seem to provide a greater return on investment. Some of our churches leave missions to our denominations and networks or partner with ministries that offer us low-cost opportunities to sponsor missionaries or projects far away. Yet does outsourcing missions come with hidden costs, perhaps at the expense of our own souls?

**We want to suggest a series of basic questions that can help churches and their leaders frame a process of discovery, design, and deployment in mission.**

In many areas of church ministry we are careful to define what we are trying to accomplish. Global outreach, however, often seems to be exempt from such attentions. But does it have to be that way? In this book, we want to suggest a series of basic questions that can help churches and their leaders frame a process of discovery, design, and deployment in mission, a process essential for a healthy, unified, dynamic missions vision that flows from thinking about missions well.

- Do our definitions matter?
- What is our mission?
- Why are we involved in missions?
- Is every Christian a missionary?
- How are missionaries to be sent?
- So what? What is at stake?
- What next? What might our next steps be?

Even as we raise these simple but challenging questions, we want to affirm churches that are doing the work of missions from the place of thinking well about missions. We have observed many churches whose elders, boards, pastors, and church missions leaders have been awakened by the Scriptures and embraced clear thinking about missions and the local church. It is highly rewarding to see churches move from passive to proactive participation in missions, no longer focused on just money and programs. May your tribe increase!

If we could place our hearts on the page, they would show you that we love God's Bride, the Church of which He is the Head and the Bridegroom of us all. He has been on mission as the missionary God ever since Genesis, exhibiting His great wisdom from before time began. We adore and glorify the miraculous way He has pursued, called, and chosen each of us to be in His family. Despite the hell-deserving sinners we are, He has opened our eyes to the good news of salvation performed in the person and work of Jesus Christ, and we have embraced Him as "the power of God unto salvation to everyone who believes" (Romans 1:16). To see Him passionately worshipped by every tribe, tongue, and nation for this incomparable act of grace is our motivation for mission.

While we will directly challenge some assumptions surrounding the growing assumption or conviction that "every Christian is a missionary and every ministry is missions," we do so in an attitude of prayer that God will give us gracious and humble hearts of expression, and that we as authors of this book will treat His Bride and each reader with all of the grace God has shown us.

Are you a missions or church leader, involved vocationally in a defined ministry role or faithfully serving Christ as you represent Him at school, work, or neighborhood? Please know that our words and concepts come without any desire to give you a "beat down" about missions in any arena. When we speak about the Church, both of us include ourselves in its brokenness and its beauty.

We realize others much more qualified than we are see some of these issues very differently. We will gladly receive feedback and dialogue, especially if it motivates our churches toward greater activity among the unreached and unengaged. We are committed to creating a conversation about this topic that will stimulate the entire Church into focused, thoughtful activity where thinking comes before doing.

We write from a North American context, though the struggles we describe may extend to other regions as well. We view the North American Church's contributions to missions with thanksgiving and are moved with joy by the results of her past vision and sacrifice as she pursued the nations with the gospel.

While we want to see the missions efforts of the North American church revitalized, we reject any notion of cultural superiority and rejoice to see the global Church take up the mantle of seeing "the whole church take the whole gospel to the whole world." The days of "from the West to the rest" are over.

We greatly appreciate much of what we have seen in the "missional" church movement of the past decade. Pastors, teachers, and ministry leaders identified with this movement have exhorted the Church and all believers to be "on mission with God" to make disciples in our own contexts. We find this commendable and praiseworthy; it offers a great hope for future generations of the Church. We embrace the exhortation of these leaders who have called us to make the discipleship process central to our obedience to the Great Commission. Careful examination of Jesus' earthly ministry makes it abundantly clear that the process of making disciples was the center of His five commissioning statements and exhibited by the enormous quantity of time He invested in His own disciples.

Yet we are concerned that an uncritical use of words, and in particular a lack of shared definition for the words mission, missions, missionary, and missional, has led to a distortion of Jesus' biblical mandate, ushered in an everything-is-missions paradigm, and moved missions from the initiation and oversight of local churches to make it the domain of individual believers responding to individualized callings. What does this imply for the future of North American missions efforts?

In defining missions poorly, past generations of Christians have sometimes made missions about money, power, and counting converts. In our own generation, a strong embrace of the everything-is-mission paradigm has sometimes led us to a humanitarian mission devoid of the gospel. While "everybody is a missionary" thinking has been intended to level the playing field for greater participation in making disciples, has this inclusivism had another, unintended result, at times? Has it led to a serious decline in interest in and support for apostolic, pioneering missions activity?

We hope that the journey of critical thought and biblical examination we are calling for will be guided by the culminating biblical picture of the Church given in Revelation 7:9-10, which describes the worship of God by a multitude from every tribe and nation. We pray this book will propel the Church into making disciples of the nations where Christ's Name is not known, adored, and worshipped. If knowing comes before doing and shapes doing, then we must think about missions well.

Yogi Berra said it well: "If you don't know where you're going, chances are you will end up somewhere else."

Let's examine what we think we know so that we can clearly define where we are going and why.

• • •

The next morning, John was having some deeper reservations about the budget meeting of the previous night. His text began:

"Pastor Steve, about the meeting last night, as Executive and Missions Pastor, I'm greatly conflicted..."

## chapter 1
# DO OUR DEFINITIONS MATTER?
## by Matthew Ellison

*Definition: The act of making something definite, distinct, or clear*

*Accuracy of language is one of the bulwarks of truth. — Anna Jameson*

*The abandonment of precision and definition is the gateway to liberalism. — John Piper*

*Do your best to present yourselves to God as one approved, a worker who has no need to be ashamed, rightly handling the word of truth. — 2 Timothy 2:15*

## WHY SHOULD WE CARE ABOUT WORDS?

WORDS HAVE MEANING. Every single day we bank on the fact that the words we speak or write convey something definite, distinct, and clear.

Imagine with me that it is Friday night, the night I take my family out to dinner. I ask my wife and kids where they would like to eat, and after a bit of playful banter, they decide on Chinese food.

After we slurp up our hot and sour soup, the entrées arrive. My daughter dives into the Kung Pao chicken, her favorite, but by the look on her face after the first bite, something is not right. Our daughter, who is severely allergic to fish, begins to experience a life-threatening reaction. She can hardly breathe and eventually passes out. Anaphylactic shock has set in. My wife dumps out her purse, rifling through its contents to find the EpiPen that we take with us no matter where we go. Carefully she inserts the pen into our daughter's thigh and injects the contents. Though the next minute seems like an eternity. Slowly but surely the reaction begins to subside.

We confront the waiter and to our absolute astonishment he flippantly responds by telling us that he considers chicken and fish, both being animal proteins, to be pretty much the same. With haste we leave the restaurant, relieved that our daughter will be okay but also shocked and confused about what just happened.

I know this fictional story is an absurd illustration. No one thinks chicken means fish, do they? Probably not. But in our postmodern world of verbal gymnastics, it has become all too common for the meaning of words to be subject to one's own interpretation. Relativism that would not be tolerated in a courtroom, bank, or insurance claim adjuster's office may be assumed in many other situations.

Sadly, when it comes to the Scriptures, too many Christians have the same high tolerance for innovative and creative interpretation and application that we find in the wider culture. So it should not surprise us that understanding of our Great Commission mandate may vary so widely. We believe, though, that this lack of concern for the accuracy of language has incredible and often terrible consequences, particularly when it comes to how we read Scripture. Paul urges us in 2 Timothy 2:15,

> "Be diligent to present yourself to God as one approved, a worker who has no need to be ashamed, rightly handling the word of truth."

Just how much confusion is there in the Church about the meaning of the Great Commission? Our combined experiences in working with hundreds of churches suggests the confusion is massive, and not just among church goers and members but church and missions leaders as well. If you were to do a quick survey of church leaders and mission-minded, missions-active people in your church, asking them just a couple of basic questions about the Great Commission, we are convinced that you would get many different and often conflicting answers. Sometimes the differences would just be semantic, but in other cases they would be fundamental.

In our missions coaching and consulting work we repeatedly encounter serious confusion and stifling disagreement among church and missions leaders about the purpose and goal of the Great Commission. Following are some questions that we have asked and are continuing to ask:

- What is the Great Commission purpose Christ gave to His Church?
- What exactly are we supposed to be doing?
- What has He called us to accomplish?
- What is the goal of the Great Commission?
- What is it that we work toward?
- What does the fulfillment of the Great Commission require of us?

Responses often reflect a quite hazy understanding of the Great Commission. And if churches are unable to state clearly and concisely their Great Commission purpose, we believe it will be nearly impossible for them to serve that purpose well.

One of the approaches that we often use to help clear the fog is to simply ask some more fundamental questions like these:

- If a church defines missions simply as "serving those in need" or "reaching lost people"—does that align with God's heartbeat for the Great Commission? Does it fully represent His heart for the whole world?

- Has Jesus left the interpretation of the Great Commission open to individual churches?

- When Jesus gave the Great Commission, did He give definite, clear, and distinct instructions? If so, what are those instructions? If so, why all the confusion?

In an article on "involving all of God's people in all of God's mission," Ed Stetzer explains the importance of God's people defining His mission:

"It will help all of God's people to be involved in all of God's mission if we will do the work of both defining the mission and choosing an appropriate cultural articulation of the mission. As Stephen Neill has said, 'When everything is mission, nothing is mission.' *The mission of God* cannot be the catch-all that includes everything from folding bulletins, to picking up trash on the highway, to coaching a ball team, to the gospel infiltrating a previously unreached people."[3]

Perhaps one of the most important questions that we should be asking when reading about the Great Commission in Scripture is this: Does God expect us to pool our good ideas and pursue the things we care about, or did Jesus intend to convey objective meaning and purpose when He gave His final marching orders?

**We would do well to think seriously about what He really meant when He commissioned us to make disciples of all the nations.**

In essence, the question we are asking is whether or not Jesus cares about definitions. If He doesn't care, then it does seem that the meaning and goal of the Great Commission are up for grabs. If He does care about words and their meaning, we would do well to think seriously about what He really meant when He commissioned us to make disciples of all the nations.

## REPEATING HISTORY?

A well-known idiom warns that those who ignore history are doomed to repeat it. President Harry Truman put it well when he said, "The only thing new in the world is the history you do not know." Most of us may know little about the momentous World Missionary Conference held more than 100 years ago in Edinburgh, Scotland for the purpose of celebrating the progress of world evangelization. This event has, however, had a significant effect on the missions thinking and activities of our era.

Consider how much had taken place in the world missions movement from 1800 to 1910, including events such as the Great Awakening in America and England, the Haystack Prayer Meeting of 1806, and the emergence of the Student Volunteer Movement for Foreign Missions, which led to the establishment of missions societies and agencies promoting a frontier missions focus. It was an era of world gospel expansion. The Edinburgh Conference would be a celebration of Great Commission progress.

To avoid possible conflict or controversies, however, the organizers determined there would be no defining theological or doctrinal discussions. Excluded from any definition or debate were the inspiration of Scripture, the Atonement, the meaning of the Great Commission, or even any discussion or defining of the nature of Christian mission. It is not surprising that churches and missions became divorced from the biblical text to assume any standard they might set for themselves. Missiologist David Hesselgrave calls this the "Edinburgh Error" because of the precedent it set for the 20th-century ecumenical missions movement:

"...The Great Commission came to be interpreted—and mission came to be defined—in accordance with prevailing interests: 'The mission is the church,' 'the church is mission,' 'The mission is the *missio Dei*, the mission of God,' 'The mission is humanization,' 'Mission is what the church does in the world,' 'The mission is everything the Church was sent to do in the world,' 'The mission is to preach the good news to the poor,' 'The mission is to build the kingdom of God and establish shalom;' and so on."[4]

Hesselgrave points out that this lack of clarity, doctrinal examination, and definition of mission by the standard of Scripture can lead—and in some circles largely has led—to the dissolution of mission:

"In addition to contributing to confusion as to the nature of mission, the Edinburgh Error contributed to the virtual demise of the great conciliar denominations of North America. At the beginning of the 20th century those denominations supplied 80 percent of the North American missionary force. At the end, they supplied no more than six percent!"[5]

More conservative mission and church leaders stayed the course, forming evangelical missions associations such as IFMA and EFMA (later merged to form MissioNexus), and in more recent years these evangelical groups have pioneered most of North America's mission efforts. Yet are we prone to the same error, leaving Scripture and definitions behind to focus on good works instead of our Great Commission? Is history repeating itself?

Under the heading "Mission Work Has Become Social Work," Scot McKnight asks, "What will become of us?" He notes,

"Missions, international missions and foreign missions are now engulfed in NGOs and global justice and water projects and infrastructure. Evangelicalism was built on evangelical church-planting pioneers. Always, or at least nearly always, such missionaries were fully engaged in church-planting as well as compassion and provisions so far as they were able. But they were there to preach and teach the gospel and win people to Christ. That's evangelicalism. A friend of mine, a missionary, told me that in the last 15 years in his corner of the missionary world he has seen not one new missionary concerned with church planting and evangelism; they are all NGO types. Giving to NGOs is on the rise; giving to church-planting is on the decline. Organize a day for evangelism training and you will be alone or close to it; organize a day for some kind of social action and you may see more than [for a] Sunday morning service."[6]

> Giving to NGOs is on the rise; giving to church-planting is on the decline.

As we examine history, what can we learn as we face that same question in our time? What will become of us? Have we drifted from our God-given mission?

So who cares about definitions? We do, and if you've read this far, we are fairly certain that you do. Most importantly, since God calls us to rightly divide the Word of Truth, we can with confidence conclude that He, too, cares about definitions.

## chapter 2
# WHAT IS OUR MISSION?

by Denny Spitters

*If the ladder is not leaning against the right wall, every step we take just gets us to the wrong place faster. — Stephen R. Covey*

*Ponder the path of your feet; then all your ways will be sure.*
*— Proverbs 4:26*

## MISSION, MISSIONS, MISSIONAL, AND THE MISSIO DEI

LOOKING TO SCRIPTURE to define missions for us is not a "slam dunk" task—but on the other hand, the Scripture's teaching is not, to use a phrase from Winston Churchill, "a riddle wrapped in a mystery inside an enigma." The canon offers more clarity than mystery or ambiguity.

The biblical text abounds with enough substantial evidence for some to conclude that taking the gospel to the nations is not only a significant and important theme in Scripture, but even the overall theme and purpose of the Bible. Missiologist Ralph Winter is often quoted as saying, "The Bible is not the basis of missions; missions is the basis of the Bible."

It's easy to reject this pithy statement as another attempt from a missions promoter trying to be heard. But is it true? Can or should our understanding of the whole Bible be filtered not only through a Christological lens but also a missiological one? Is this an approach we must consider for understanding the Bible's metanarrative, its over-arching theme?

My own thinking about this has changed over the years. I once believed the Bible was the basis of missions, looking for biblical passages, stories, and verses that were about missions (or supported my ideas about missions) with a goal of becoming "missions minded." But the Bible's purpose, to my mind, was to be a how-to manual for living. Missions was not essential or fundamental; it was more of an add-on.

> **But the Bible's purpose, to my mind, was to be a how-to manual for living. Missions was not essential or fundamental; it was more of an add-on.**

## THE MISSIONARY HEART OF GOD

In the booklet *Gospel Meditations for Missions,* Pastor Chris Anderson challenges such thinking. He says,

> "Missions isn't an addendum that was stapled onto normal Christianity. It's at the heart of Christianity because it's at the heart of God Himself. God is the Great Missionary of the Scriptures."[7]

How many of us see God in such terms, as the great cross-cultural missionary of the Scriptures? Yet Jesus was sent from the culture of God's kingdom and came to live among us. Anderson explains in a simple overview how God as the great missionary—from the Fall in the garden of Eden, to Abraham's promise, to establishment of Israel as a nation, to the coming of the Messiah as King, to His Second Coming—is seeking worshippers who will display His glory among the nations. God is on a mission; God is all about mission. We will look at this in greater detail below.

Maybe the most succinct statement of God's mission, outside of Scripture, may be this one found in John Piper's book *Let the Nations Be Glad:* "Missions exists because worship doesn't."[8] That God seeks to be known and worshipped makes missions the basis of the Bible as the story of God working out His redemptive purpose through sending His Son who is to be declared among the nations.

Words like those of Ralph Winter and John Piper propelled me to change my perception and perspective toward Scripture and the Bible's central theme. Rather than approaching it as a collection of stories to pick and choose for self-help, I began to visualize it as one book with one main character, theme, and purpose.

## MISSION WORDS IN THE BIBLE

Does the Bible provide any clear definitions for *mission, missions,* and *missionaries*? If these words aren't even in the Bible, how can we expect the Bible to tell us what they mean? These are critical questions, and in answering them it might be helpful for us to remember that many of the words we use for the historical Church's core doctrines and key concepts are not explicitly found in scripture, including our concepts of the Trinity, evangelism, sacraments, and church planting. Yet sound biblical exegesis supports our understanding of these concepts and show them to be more than just human constructions.

Eckhard Schnabel is considered one of the world's leading experts on missions in the New Testament and author of two 1000-page volumes on early Christian mission as well as the 500-page work *Paul the Missionary.* He says decisively,

> "The argument that the word *mission* does not occur in the New Testament is incorrect. The Latin verb *mittere* corresponds to the Greek verb *apostellein,* which occurs 136 times in the New Testament (97 times in the Gospels, used both for Jesus having been 'sent' by God and for the Twelve being 'sent' by Jesus)."[9]

So maybe our words about missions are in the Bible, and the core meaning has to do with being "sent." But since definitions matter, how do we approach the multiple ways these words are used in the Church?

## FOUR COMPETING WORDS

The terms *missio Dei, mission, missions,* and *missional* are used in many ways, and often not defined or clearly distinguished. But these terms are as different from one another as they are related and even interconnected to one another. Keeping Schnabel's observations in mind, let's take a closer look.

- *Missio Dei* translates as "mission of God," and is used to signify all that God does in the world and all that He is doing to accomplish His objective, the complete exaltation of the fame of His name: "I will be exalted among the nations, I will be exalted in the earth" (Psalm 46:10).

- *Mission* has a secular meaning; it often refers to either an underlying purpose (as in the term "mission statement") or a specific campaign or objective (as in a military or diplomatic mission). But it is also used to define the scope of all that God has given His Church to accomplish within the *missio Dei*; it may include all that God has called the Church to do in the world.

- *Missional,* the most modern of the four terms, is an adjective used primarily to distinguish the ministry of the Church that happens beyond its four walls (as opposed to caring for its own). Some now use the term *missional* where they may have previously used *mission* or *missions.* This term has also been co-opted to describe a specific, progressive style of church which is intentionally outreach-oriented (a missional church or a missional community).

- *Missions* may be used as a synonym, perhaps a clunky or outdated one, for any of the terms above, and our British brothers and sisters are among those who prefer the more graceful term "mission" without necessarily a switch in meaning between the two. But *missions* also has a narrower meaning. It is used to refer to the work of the Church in reaching across cultural, religious, ethnic and geographic barriers to advance the work of making disciples of all nations, a process described in Romans 10:14-15 among other places:

> "How then will they call on him in whom they have not believed? How will they believe in him of whom they have never heard? And how will they hear without someone preaching? And how are they to preach unless they are sent? As it is written, 'How beautiful are the feet of those who preach the good news!'"

Missiologist Gary Corwin, in article "MissionS: Why the 'S' Is Still Important," compares these four terms and one more: "In addition, establishing churches among those people groups and communities where Christ is least known has been distinguished over the last several decades as what *frontier missions* is all about."[10]

**Defining words in a postmodern era can make any of us a lightning rod for debate, division, and controversy.**

Are all four terms needed? Despite the overlapping meanings, says Corwin, each has an important, particular emphasis, and when they are properly understood, each serves a useful purpose. The problem comes when the terms are used in ways for which they are inadequate and these emphases are lost:

> "To say, for example, that either the *missio Dei* and the mission of the church is synonymous, or that the mission of the church is all that one needs to focus on or be concerned about, runs the very real risk of simply defining everything as mission."[11]

Defining words in a post-modern era can make any of us a lightning rod for debate, division, and controversy. Yet how the Church understands its mission is of monumental importance as we seek to be obedient to God's Word.

## FIVE GREAT COMMISSIONING STATEMENTS

Jesus gives us a number of commands to obey in the New Testament, and these include five commissioning statements that form the foundation for our understanding of missions: John 20:21, Matthew 28:18-20, Mark 16:15, Luke 24:44-49, and Acts 1:8. In these passages, and in fact from Genesis to Revelation, we see the central themes of "being sent" and "sending" as two interwoven fibers that make up the thread of missions activity. These two themes are central to thinking about missions well. They bring clarity to the process of defining God's mission for the Church. These two themes help guide us as we choose what Steven Covey would call "the wall against which to lean our ladder."

In his book *Commissioned: What Jesus Wants You to Know As You Go,* Marvin Newell writes about the compelling unity of these five statements, claiming that they contain all the essential ingredients for successful mission. Newell also makes the case that these commissions were given on five different occasions, in five different places, and each with its own emphasis.[12]

John 20:21 takes place immediately after the Resurrection, with the events described in Mark 16:15, Matthew 28:18-20, and Luke 24:44-49 coming next. Finally, Acts 1:8 takes place 40 days after the Resurrection, immediately before the Ascension. "Without question these five mission statements of Jesus make up the missional Magna Carta of the Church, from its inception, for today, and into the future," says Newell.[13]

He further describes their emphases as follows:[14]

• The Model: "As the Father has sent me..." John 20:21

- The Magnitude: "go into all the world... to the whole creation" Mark 16:15

- The Methodology: "...make disciples of all nations..." Matthew 28:18-20

- The Message: "...repentance and forgiveness of sins..." Luke 24:44-49

- The Means: "you will receive power... Jerusalem, Judea, Samaria..." Acts 1:8

Within this biblical narrative, who is sending and who is being sent? To answer this question well, it is imperative to begin with the alignment of our thoughts and attitudes to God's master kingdom blueprint plan, the commission of His Church—starting with the end in mind.

## GOD THE MISSIONARY

Revelation 7:9-10 provides the picture of the end of the mission. John's Isaiah-esque vision ushers us right to the final scene of the triumphant reality: the enthroned King is adored and worshipped by people from every tribe, language, and people. The divine initiation of this mission centers on the Messiah first mentioned in Genesis 3:15, making God both the sender and the sent one. God has woven this thread through biblical history for every age. The Genesis 12:1-3 blessing and commissioning of Abram is a key moment in God's mission, one in which He not only shares His purpose with Abram but entrusts him with its future, saying, "in you all the families of the earth will be blessed."

This seems to be the central plot and theme of the Bible—it is the story of a missionary God who is both the "sent" one and the one "sending out." God has a mission. He Himself is the main character of the story—engaged as initiator and participant in the grand design of redeeming the greatest tragedy in history, the Fall of man, as He brings glory to Himself. He made the way for us to be reconciled and brought back into intimate relationship with Him by breaking the cycle of sin and judgment. God initiates by "sending out" the hope of redemption, His Son Jesus Christ. Jesus directly validates this plan and purpose in John 17: "And this is eternal life, that they know you, the only true God, and Jesus Christ whom you have sent" (John 17:3).

What an incredible amazing God, whose intentional design and purpose both provides His people with the final framing picture and supplies the means to its fulfillment through the person and work of His Son—the One being sent from the God who is sending. This is the framework we are called to work within when Jesus said, "Go into all the world and make disciples of all nations." This story of redemption is at the heart of the *missio Dei*. But is there a difference between the mission of God and the mission of the church?

## WHAT IS THE MISSION OF THE CHURCH?

Can the mission of the church even be defined? Some contend that there is no possibility for coherence or agreement within the Church on either the meaning or the concept of the Church's mission and no single theology for missions, but several different, valid approaches. Others claim the language of mission and missions is so flawed and weighed down with history that it should be eliminated or completely redefined. To focus on what's wrong or negative with missions and missions language has become a great emphasis in missiology—perhaps unsurprising given that deconstructionism is the modus operandi of our day. We see this approach expressed by influential missiologist and theologian David Bosch in his book *Transforming Mission:*

> "Ultimately, mission remains indefinable.... The most we can hope for is to formulate some approximations of what mission is all about."[15]

If it could be identified, Bosch contends, we could not apply what mission was then to ourselves today, and so we must "prolong the logic of the ministry of Jesus and the early church in an imaginative way and context."

Keith Ferdinando tackles such a claim directly in his article "Mission: A Problem with Definition," asserting that such thinking leads to a relativist and subjectivist approach. In contrast,

"One could argue that the Bible offers a fundamentally coherent picture of the mission of a God who, from Adam's first disobedience, pursues rebellious humanity to redeem a people, a purpose whose realization is portrayed in John's vision of 'a great multitude that no one could count, from every nation, tribe, people and language, standing before the throne and in front of the Lamb' (Revelation 7:9). That mission he now carries out through his church as it makes disciples of Jesus Christ."

Ferdinando repudiates Bosch's biblical exposition:

"[Bosch's] hermeneutic alongside the emphasis on biblical diversity risks cutting mission free from any control by the biblical text and surrendering it to the creativity of interpreters. ... Bosch's thesis thus provides a theoretical justification for the loss of consensus with reference to 'mission'; indeed it makes a virtue of ambiguity, for mission becomes a term constantly seeking a meaning.[16]

## ARE THE MISSION OF GOD AND THE MISSION OF THE CHURCH IDENTICAL?

We return to the question, "Are the mission of God and the mission of the Church the same?" Is the Church's mission everything God's mission is, or are there distinctions and differences? Here we see the influence of Christopher Wright, whose books *Mission of God: Unlocking the Bible's Grand Narrative* and *The Mission of God's People* tackle this question.

We find much to agree with in *The Mission of God.* Wright supports the concept of reading the Bible within the structure of its grand narrative. Rather than shining a spotlight on various parts of the inspired Scripture to discover what missions is, he fully asserts:

> "The God who walks the paths of history through the pages of the Bible pins a mission statement to every signpost on the way."[17]

He tackles postmodernism head on:

> "What we have to offer, I contend, is a missional hermeneutic of the Bible: The Bible got there before postmodernity was dreamed of—the Bible which glories in diversity and celebrates multiple human cultures, the Bible which builds its most elevated theological claims on utterly particular and sometimes very local events, the Bible which sees everything in relational, not abstract terms, and the Bible which does the bulk of its work through the medium of stories. All of these features of the Bible—cultural, local, relational, narrative—are welcome to the postmodern mind."[18]

He is clear that we must look to Scripture for our understanding of missions:

> "...not just that the Bible contains a number of texts which happen to provide a rationale for missionary endeavor but that the whole Bible is itself a 'missional' phenomenon."[19]

Even as Wright aggressively addresses postmodern thinking with the Bible, however, he blurs biblical distinctions about the mission of God and the mission of the Church.

> "It is of course not just a single narrative, like a river with only one channel. It is rather a complex mixture of all kinds of smaller narratives, many of them rather self-contained,

with all kinds of other material embedded within them—more like a delta."[20]

Wright advances this concept by equating "all that God is doing in his great purpose for the whole of creation," with "all that he calls us to do in cooperation with that purpose," further expanding,

"And it seems to me there are as many kinds of missions as there are kinds of sciences—probably far more in fact. And in the same way, in the variety of missions God has entrusted to his church as a whole, it is unseemly for one kind of mission to dismiss another out of a superiority complex, or to undervalue itself as 'not real mission' out of an inferiority complex. The body image has powerful resonance here too. That is why I also dislike the old knockdown line that sought to ring-fence the word 'mission' for specifically cross-cultural sending of missionaries for evangelism: 'If everything is mission, then nothing is mission.' It would seem more biblical to say, 'If everything is mission... everything is mission.'"[21]

> **The Church was given a very specific mandate from Jesus and passed on to the disciples at His ascension; the Church is by no means equipped to carry out all that God does on the earth or in the universe.**

Though Wright seems to conclude that everything is mission, he provides little biblical hermeneutic to support his case. In our view, it is not "unseemly" nor "superior" to clarify the differences between important ministries of the Church (such as mercy ministry) and missions outreach, in light of the solid biblical precedent of Jesus' commissioning statements.

The Church was given a very specific mandate from Jesus, passed on to the disciples at His ascension; the Church is by no means equipped to carry out all that God does on the earth or in the universe. Though the mission of God, a divine gargantuan task, is assumed by Wright to be given to the Church, none of the early disciples or church fathers seem to have been occupied with this idea or this task.

Wright seems concerned that a Great Commission-based understanding of missions is too narrow. His view, in contrast, is surprisingly broad:

"Holistic mission, then, is not truly holistic if it includes only human beings (even if it includes them holistically!) and excludes the rest of the creation for whose reconciliation Christ shed his blood (Colossians 1:20). Those Christians show they have responded to God's call to serve him through serving his nonhuman creatures in ecological projects are engaged in a specialized form of mission that has its rightful place within the broad framework of all that God's mission has as its goal."[22]

It is a given that missions is not one-dimensional proclamation divorced from demonstration. Yet does Wright's position go to too far in saying that creation care is an arm of holistic missions validated by "its rightful place within the broad framework of all the God's mission has as its goal"? Parameters for the care of creation were given in Genesis 1:28: to be fruitful and increase in number, fill and subdue it, rule over fish, birds, and every creature on the earth. We would assert that God's reconciliation of creation will not occur in the preservation of the earth through the endeavors of holistic ministry; God's reconciliation of the earth will be its purification by fire and the creation of a new one (Revelation 21:1). Becoming a "missionary to creation" may reflect on the renewal-of-nature theme in the *missio Dei,* but can only be embraced by stretching the mission of the Church far beyond the focus provided in the parameters of Scripture. Where will we draw the line? Climate change missions, animal rescue missions, gender identification missions? Wright's "delta" concept galvanized by the altruism of the human heart would know no boundaries; it seems to go too far.

For many in evangelicalism today, God's mission of reconciling everything to Himself and the mission of the church are one and the same. Clearly the two must be connected. But we assert that they are not the same. God's scope is from eternity to eternity. As His disciples, we have a specific sub-plot in the redemption story and a distinct role under the authority of Christ and the commission of His Church.

Modern missions history shows us this: Whenever the primacy of disciple making and church planting have been replaced with efforts to eradicate the world's evil systems, diseases, and oppressions, the global disciple-making activities of the church have foundered. And, on the flip side, we can observe that the regions of the world that have seen the greatest democratic reforms and social welfare in the last 300 years are those where missionaries focused *most* on personal conversion through the preaching of the gospel and *least* on social transformation. We do not oppose social transformation and holistic ministry but we do not believe they are the goal. Making disciples who birth the local church is the key to both evangelism and social transformation. Compassion ministry as missions—without the gospel as its primary vehicle for existence and expression—easily lapses into little more than humanistic accomplishment.

## CENTRALITY OF DISCIPLESHIP AND THE NATIONS

The historical, orthodox view of missions which has as its bulls-eye, its innermost circle, the making of disciples, has served the Church well—as is evidenced by the rapid worldwide expansion of Christianity during the past millennium. Careful observation of the book of Acts reveals that the primacy of making disciples of all nations and teaching them to obey all that Jesus had commanded them was the path the Church was to follow. Ferdinando emphasizes,

"...There is a distinctive apostolic mission taking place in Acts which is an expression of explicit obedience to the great commission. Its focus is on winning people to the faith and to the way of life which that faith produces, and its method is proclamation of the word of Christ. It is also true that Acts portrays believers engaging in social action—caring for widows, for example—but that is a consequence of apostolic mission rather than its substance: it is one of the forms—albeit a vitally important form—which faithful discipleship takes among those who have responded to the gospel. Nevertheless, it does not have the same place as the making of disciples itself, and this relates to the obvious fact that Christian social engagement depends on the existence of Christians, and there would be none if disciples were not made."[23]

## A CASE FOR SETTING PRIORITIES

Theologian and missiologist Christopher Little describes two positions held by evangelicals as "holism" and "prioritism." Those who view mission holistically see evangelism, disciple-making, and church planting as no more important than ministries of social justice and humanitarianism, while those who hold the prioritist position say that they are. And, Little says, "Those who advance evangelism as the priority in the mission of the church are now in the clear minority among self-described evangelicals."[24] While few evangelicals want to see a dichotomy between word and deed—believing the church should minister through both—the author points out that one cannot logically claim that both "there are priorities" and "there are no priorities" in mission; "One must be true and the other false; there are no other options. Hence, a choice must be made."[25]

"The debate, has, in fact, been going on for a long time. So why not just agree to disagree and move forward? Simply because the stakes are too high to overlook, set aside, or not contest. These include, first and foremost, the eternal destiny of the unevangelized. Since they are the ones who have the most to lose, their concerns should be front and center."[26]

Little is also concerned that Christians in the West now give more to relief and development and other humanitarian causes than to foreign missions and are redefining the terms *gospel, kingdom,* and *missions* in unprecedented ways. These shifts in missions are largely unchallenged, but he sees them as a clear case of "mission drift."[27]

## STAYING ON THE PATH

A scene from *The Desolation of Smaug,* the second film of the Hobbit series, gives us a vivid picture. The film follows Bilbo Baggins as he accompanies Thorin Oakenshield and his fellow dwarves on a quest to reclaim the Lonely Mountain from the gold-addicted dragon Smaug. Halfway to their destination, their guide Gandalf the Grey must release them for their journey through the enchanted and degrading Mirkwood Forest and sternly warns them:

"This is not the Greenwood of old, the very air of the forest is heavy with illusion that will seek to enter your mind and lead you astray ... You must stay on the path, do not leave it. If you do, you'll never find it again. No matter what may come, stay on the path!"

At first they manage to follow it faithfully but as they get deeper into the forest they find it harder to breathe. The illusions and enchantment of Mirkwood quickly cloud and alter their judgment and thinking. They stumble and pick their way deeper and deeper into a growing veil of haziness and fog when suddenly—panic stricken—they realize they have lost the path.

We are unapologetic and ardent activists for a narrow, Great-Commission-focused definition of missions that will that keep the Church on the path of making disciples of all nations. Maintaining a narrow definition of missions will be a more useful tool for the Church in fulfilling her mission, and the overall thrust of Scripture readily supports this emphasis.

Offering a prophetic and practical exhortation, missiologist and mission mobilizer Jeff Lewis says:

"The local church is a community of disciples of the King, liberated from the slavery of self, called to be fully engaged in the redemptive mission among the nations (both locally and globally), and they are charged with the nurturing and training of God's children to be disciplers of the nations. The Church must rediscover her mission and the responsibility of developing kids, teenagers, and adults fully equipped to disciple the nations both locally and to the ends of the earth."[28]

To cross the barriers that missions requires, we must bring significant focus and special emphasis in the Church to making disciples resulting in churches. Without this regular and specific emphasis on "making disciples of the nations," the needs and outreach of the local church will always, quite naturally, receive the greatest attention of our efforts and attention, while the voices of those with no access become a distant memory until next year's "Missions Sunday."

A sound biblical missions definition is crucial to the future of the evangelical Church. Defining missions in our relativistic, pluralistic era requires that we are committed to walking the path of God's redemptive mission, culminating in the collective worship of the Lamb by all nations, peoples, tribes, and tongues. That is the bedrock path of missions to which we, His Bride, are called. No matter what process we use to define and carry out missions activity, this is the path our boots must travel.

## chapter 3

# WHY ARE WE INVOLVED IN MISSIONS?

by Matthew Ellison

*"And I heard the voice of the Lord saying, 'Whom shall I send, and who will go for us?' Then I said, 'Here I am! Send me.'"*
— Isaiah 6:8

*"Worship is the fuel and goal of missions. Missions begins and ends in worship."* — John Piper

## FOUNDATIONAL MOTIVES FOR GLOBAL MINISTRY

I T ONLY MAKES SENSE to ask: Why should we go through all the effort, trouble, and expense of leaving home to preach the gospel all around the world? After all, whether we go ourselves or send others, crossing cultures to serve among the world's least reached and forgotten peoples is an enormously complex process that requires an unbelievable amount of work and sacrifice. And then there are the needs of lost people right on our doorstep...

In light of those realities, why missions? A reexamination of our motivations may help us set biblical priorities and stay the course. This chapter explores five of our foundational motives for global ministry.

## I. BECAUSE GOD'S HEART BEATS FOR THE NATIONS

On how many different occasions did Jesus give the Great Commission? My friend and missions mentor Robertson

McQuilkin used to tell me that no one ever gets that question right. As we saw in chapter two, the New Testament has five "great commissioning" passages, five reports of what Jesus taught to different audiences and on different occasions: Matthew 28:18-20, Mark 16:15, Luke 24:44-49, John 20:21, and Acts 1:8. The Luke 24 passage suggests that these commands also stand on a biblical foundation that goes back much further. It warrants a closer look.

Luke tells us that Jesus and His disciples were in the upper room when He "opened up their minds to understand the Scriptures" (Luke 24:45). That, by the way, is our prayer for this book: that Christ would use it to open minds to understand the Scriptures. Jesus showed them passages about His death and Resurrection and He taught them that repentance and remission of sins must be preached in His Name to all nations.

Now, where in the Scriptures did Jesus turn to teach His followers that the gospel must be preached to all nations? To the Gospels, or the Epistles? Of course not. According to verse 44, He took them to the Law, the Prophets, and the Psalms. He took them to the Old Testament. Here's the point: though Great Commission thinking pervades the New Testament, God's missionary heart that beats for the nations didn't just suddenly appear at that point; it is unmistakably enunciated throughout the Old Testament, too. And then, between the Resurrection and the Ascension, Jesus pulls the threads together and repeats what we might call a Great Commission at least five times.

In those first six weeks following the resurrection, Jesus appeared to His disciples over and over and He taught them many things. We don't have any record that He repeated any theme, except for two:

1. The Resurrection
2. The Great Commission

The Great Commission was our Commanding Officer's marching orders. You might say it was His burning ambition.

The Great Commission is central to Scripture, central to God's heart, and central to God's thinking and activity. And the commission is not solely about making disciples wherever we find ourselves; it's also about taking the gospel to all the world, the whole creation (Mark 16:15), all nations (Matthew 28:18-20), and even to the ends of the earth (Acts 1:8).

I have heard it said that if we could hear God's heartbeat, we'd hear His heart beating for the nations. So if we love God's Word, if we love God's fame, and if we are committed to magnifying His Name above all things, we cannot, we must not, be indifferent to the nations: all the nations (*panta ta ethne*). And a close look of scripture suggests this term refers not to nation-states like the 194 or so countries in our world today, but to families, clans, or cultures. Our world is home to more than 16,000 groups with distinct languages and cultures, each beloved by God and made for His glory.

Why missions? Because God's heart beats for the nations.

## 2. BECAUSE SALVATION IS FOUND ONLY IN JESUS

If men could be saved by any other means other than through Jesus, then, according to Paul, not only did Jesus die in vain (Galatians 2:21) but we who preach Him preach in vain. And missionaries? If there is another way, they need to find a new line of work.

Yet according to Acts 4:12, salvation is found in Him only: "And there is salvation in no one else, for there is no other name under heaven given among men by which we must be saved." Notice two very important phrases in this passage:

- No name under heaven: not just no other name in Israel, but no other name under heaven (and the whole world is under heaven).

- No name given among men: not just among Jews, but among men generically (referring to all mankind).

Isn't that what Jesus said in John 14:6? "I am the way, and the truth, and the life. No one comes to the Father except through me."

## IN THE TEMPLE OF THE DEAD

Several years ago I was in Thiruvalla in the Indian state of Kerala and visited a place locally known as the Temple of the Dead. I noticed a Hindu priest sweeping the courtyard and felt compelled to have a conversation with him. After spending some time just getting to know him a bit, I felt that I could move the conversation to spiritual matters. After all, he was a priest and we were in the courtyard of a Hindu temple. So I asked him, "Friend, has Hinduism satisfied you? Do you have hope beyond this life?"

He paused for a moment, and with empty eyes that gave away the emptiness in his soul, he responded, "No, I am not satisfied by Hinduism and I have no hope beyond this life..."

This was a priest, mind you, not just a practitioner of Hinduism, but an apparent holy man of the Hindu faith, and he confessed his emptiness and hopelessness apart from Christ.

Why missions? Because those who don't have Christ will never find true peace in this life. Worse yet, if they die apart from Him, they will face an eternity of conscious terrifying torment in hell.

## IS HELL REAL?

This question has been debated by Christians for over two millennia. Several years ago another book came out disputing the reality of hell, Rob Bell's *Love Wins*. A subsequent barrage of commentary about the topic ensued once again. Bell thinks he knows this answer. Or should I say, he thinks we can't know for certain, because he believes that the biblical discussion of salvation is contradictory. This incited many evangelicals to contend in the public arena that Jesus Christ is man's only hope and that the eternal punishment for not believing in Him is conscious, eternal, terrifying torment.

I thank God for those who took this stand; it is my stand, and, more importantly it is the historical biblical position. I must confess, however, that the debate caused serious consternation in my heart not over whether or not hell is real but rather why so many evangelicals who claim to believe in hell and strongly defend the doctrine can seem to pay so little attention to the unreached who sit in darkness and under the shadow of death.

In his landmark book *Let the Nations Be Glad,* John Piper poses three questions and provides biblical answers:

1.  Will anyone experience eternal conscious torment under God's wrath?

2.  Is the work of Christ the necessary means provided by God for eternal salvation?

3.  Is it necessary for people to hear of Christ in order to be eternally saved?

Piper writes, "Biblical answers to these three questions are crucial because in each case a negative answer would seem to cut a nerve of urgency in the missionary cause." He goes on to unpack biblical passage after biblical passage, relying on Scripture's intrinsic authority to tell us yet again that the answer to all three of these questions is a resounding *yes.*[29]

Of course he is right: a negative answer to any of these questions would cut a nerve of urgency in the missionary cause. But when one considers that today there are still more than 6,700 unreached people groups,[30] nearly half of them unengaged by Christians seeking to share the gospel with them, we may conclude that evangelicals possess little if any sense of urgency for God's missionary cause.

The global population of evangelicals tops 335 million, for a ratio of more than 100,000 evangelicals for each unengaged group.[31] When we follow the money we see .01 percent of the personal income of Christians ($1 out of every $10,000) is given to global foreign missions of all kinds.[32]

If all of the resources needed to send and support an army of Christ-centered ambassadors to the nations is already in the Church, why do we see such minimal commitment?

Our lack of commitment to Christ's marching orders to make disciples of all nations indeed begs the question, do we really believe in the reality and the eternality of hell? The evidence seems to say that we don't. If we do, then something is horribly wrong, for our doctrine is not being demonstrated in our demeanor.

Why missions? Because salvation is found only in Jesus.

## 3. BECAUSE OUR CHURCHES CAN'T AFFORD NOT TO DO MISSIONS

Australian Archbishop David Penman once said,

> "I do not believe any local congregation, no matter what its situation, can afford to deprive itself of the encouragement and nourishment that comes by sending missionaries and reading about missionaries beyond their church walls."[33]

Many churches today are lacking in the spiritual vitality that could be theirs. That they do not know the joy of being part of the "family business." God the Father, through Christ, makes us His sons and daughters, and then, wonder of wonders, calls us to join Him in the fulfillment of history's greatest movement.

### ONE CHURCH'S JOURNEY

Several years ago, I had the privilege of walking alongside Rockpointe Community Church in Sterling Heights, Michigan as they formed a strategic missions vision which included a key effort to reach an unreached people. They would eventually launch a church-based team of three families to plant churches in Senegal, West Africa.

Some context is necessary to fully appreciate their remarkable journey. The year was 2010; the US economy was still reeling from the 2009 market crash and they lived in what seems to be the epicenter of the financial woes in the United States. Many people at Rockpointe were without jobs. Layoffs of church staff were also under consideration.

It was in this context that they begin forging their global vision and strategy. Amazingly, the vision was not only fully funded by the congregation, it also began to transform the lives of the people of Rockpointe in unexpected ways. They called the vision Everyone Dakar, the idea being that everyone at Rockpointe had a role to play in it. (Notice how that differs from saying "everyone is a missionary.")

Pastor Randy Tamko reported some of the key ways the vision has changed the church: They now look at their local context differently. He has also seen them change the way they approach their own lives in light of the sacrifice they and their missionaries are making for the sake of those on the other side of the world.

"People began viewing Detroit and the entire metro area and the Muslim community in a way that prior to I don't think we were conscious of or would have looked at as closely. For the longest time I've wanted everyone to share ministry instead of just investing in a professional class [of missionaries]. We've done better at that than most churches have done.

"This has taken us way beyond that, though, because in these people making their choices and their sacrifices, stepping out like they have, and step out like they have in the prime of their career track, everyone's has had to face that and deal with that, and say, ' 'Why would they do that? And if they're doing that because God's calling them to it, what does that mean for me?' And that's just changed everyone's approach to how they look at life, and this whole area, and I think it's being poured back into the entire city of Detroit.

"We have made the most significant contribution to global missions than we've ever done as a church. The interesting thing, though, is the impact that has had on us as a church. And not just us as a church but on how everyone views their mission here in the Detroit area. This launch has had more impact locally and within us as a people than it has yet to have overseas."[34]

Did you get that? Their engagement in God's work of discipling all nations changed them as a church, even more than it has changed Dakar (so far). Stories about generous giving, people engaging in local outreach in new ways, and people reaching out to Muslims in their backyard abound. Pastor Randy said that Rockpointe's participation in reaching a people group at the ends of the earth changed how people look at life and that this overflowed into their local ministries too.

Rockpointe experienced what J.D. Greear called (in a book of the same title) "gaining by losing."[35] They sent some of their best people and most significant resources out of the building—way out of the building—and the end result was not a loss, but a spiritual increase, not only for the kingdom but for their church as well.

Rockpointe's story is not unique. I have seen church after church radically adopt God's heart for the nations by embracing world missions and as a result be nourished and encouraged by God in ways they had not anticipated.

I believe that some of the sweetest and most profound joy available to God's children this side of heaven comes when we sacrificially participate in His mission to make disciples of all nations. Missions brings life to the nations. Missions bring life to the Church.

Why missions? Because our churches can't afford not to do missions.

## 4. BECAUSE WE ARE CALLED TO KNOW GOD AND MAKE HIM KNOWN

In Isaiah 6:1-8 we have what I consider one of the most significant mission passages in all of Scripture. Here we see what it was that ignited a prophet and set him ablaze to know God and to make God known.

"In the year that King Uzziah died I saw the Lord sitting upon a throne, high and lifted up; and the train of his robe filled the temple. Above him stood the seraphim. Each had six wings: with two he covered his face, and with two he covered his feet, and with two he flew. And one called to another and said:

"'Holy, holy, holy is the LORD OF HOSTS; the whole earth is full of his glory!'

"And the foundations of the thresholds shook at the voice of him who called, and the house was filled with smoke. And I said: 'Woe is me! For I am lost; for I am a man of unclean lips, and I dwell in the midst of a people of unclean lips; for my eyes have seen the King, the LORD OF HOSTS!'

"Then one of the seraphim flew to me, having in his hand a burning coal that he had taken with tongs from the altar. And he touched my mouth and said: 'Behold, this has touched your lips; your guilt is taken away, and your sin atoned for.'

"And I heard the voice of the Lord saying, 'Whom shall I send, and who will go for us?' Then I said, 'Here I am! Send me.'"

Isaiah's commission into the ministry began with what A.W. Tozer calls a crisis of encounter,[36] a definitive life experience. He will never be the same again. He saw the Lord, and the word he uses is, Adoni, a term of reference for the Supreme Lord of all who is over all.

The text says that Isaiah didn't have this vision of Jesus until Uzziah died. Bible scholars speculate, but I wonder if the prophet may have been too focused on the king instead of the King of kings. After all, Uzziah's reign had ushered in a time of national prosperity and material abundance. Maybe Isaiah's heart was fragmented, while God seems to reserve the depths of discovery of His nature to those whose hearts are completely His.

In Whatever Happened to Worship, A.W. Tozer suggests that the prophet had become familiar with the good things that God had created, but did not yet know God's presence.[37] Could it be that a great many people who go to church are familiar with the good things that God has made, but have never experienced His holiness or known His presence?

If we want to make our lives count for the sake of God's purposes and for the sake of eternity, then we must have a sharp and stunning encounter with Christ. We must see Him. But we'll never see Him as He really is until our hearts are His alone—until He is enthroned within us. Is there anything in our lives that is competing for God's attention and His affection? Is there anything that is clouding our vision of Him? By the grace of God and the aid of the Holy Spirit, it must be removed so we can see the Lord as He really is.

Take careful notice of the unusual supernatural creatures that attended Isaiah's crisis of encounter: seraphim. Notice their unusual anatomy; they have six wings. Four wings are for reverence and worship, covering their faces and feet, while two wings are for service—to fly around and do the Lord's will. These creatures are to care more about worship than service. Worship must come first!

As John Piper says, worship is both the fuel and goal of missions. Missions begins and ends in worship. And where zeal for worship is weak, zeal for missions will be weak.[38]

It's another way of saying that we do not commend what we do not cherish. If you want to find someone that is alive to the glory of God and is passionately pursuing God's mission purposes, then find someone that is centered on Christ and passionate about exalting Him.

Listen closely to the creatures' cries to one another; they say, "Holy, holy, holy is the Lord of hosts; the whole earth is full of his glory!" Their voices are so loud that the very threshold of heaven shakes. Their exclamation is focused on the glory of God. This is what the Great Commission is all about—the glory of God that will one day cover the earth the way the waters cover the seas.

As Tozer says, a true encounter with God will be permanent and life-changing: "The experience may have been brief, but the results will be evident in the life of the person touched as long as he or she lives."[39]

Seeing the holiness of Christ also made Isaiah conscious of his own sin in a whole new way. He finally had an accurate vision of himself. In the end this moved him to silence and then confession. Isaiah agrees with God; God, you are glorious. God, I am a sinner; God, I've missed it. I've heard it said that the man who thinks he has something to offer God, save his broken life, is not fit for service. If I want to be used by God, I must come to Him with open, empty hands. The irony is that the one thing He wants is the one thing I truly have to give, a broken life. Those of us who want to be mighty for God must first be undone and unraveled.

If the story ended here, we would be in some deep trouble. Not only is our God holy, but He is also merciful. Isaiah's sincere confession led to an immediate cleansing. His fearful trembling now becomes joyful trembling. Not only does God remove his sin but also his guilt. Such a work of grace is vital for effective ministry and effective missions work. Only when Isaiah was cleansed did he hear the call of the Lord.

Isaiah was told He would be sent to people who would not listen, but he accepted his calling anyway. Our commission is somewhat different. Matthew 24:14 assures us that the gospel of the kingdom will be preached throughout the whole world as a testimony to all the nations. That being the case, we can embrace our mission to make disciples of all nations with a great sense of expectancy and excitement.

Why missions? Because, like Isaiah, we are called to know God—to experience His holiness and presence and to know our own brokenness and His mercy for us. We are to know Him and make Him known.

## 5. BECAUSE THE LAMB DESERVES HIS REWARD

Perhaps you've heard of Count Nicolas Ludwig Von Zinzendorf.[40] Born in Germany in 1700 to a very wealthy family, he came to Christ while still a young man and eventually founded a Christian community called "Hernhut," meaning the Lord's watch.

Hernhut eventually became part of the Moravian Church Movement which is best known for its unbridled missionary zeal. True to their name, the Lord's Watch, a "round the clock" prayer watch began in 1727, the year the community was established. Prayer was fundamental to them from the start. This prayer watch lasted unbroken for 100 years. Historians cite that various members of the initial 300 covenanted with one another to make sure that every hour of every day was covered in prayer. They prayed for the nations.

By 1792, 65 years later, the prayer watch still intact, and the Moravians had sent 300 missionaries to the unreached people of the North America, the West Indies, Greenland, Turkey, and Lapland.

What was driving them to be so radically committed to making Jesus known among the nations? It was an overwhelming passion for the Savior and corresponding reverence for the blood that He shed to purchase people for God from every tribe, tongue, and nation.

When Zinzendorf finished university, he had taken a cultural sight-seeing trip through Europe. Something very unexpected happened on this trip happened that would change not only his life trajectory but the eternal destinies of peoples all over the world. In an art museum in Düsseldorf, he came upon a painting by Domenico Feti titled *Ecce Homo,* Latin for *Behold the Man.* It was a portrait of Christ before Pilate being presented to the crowds after being beaten by the Romans, the crown of thorns pressed down on his head and blood running down his face. Beneath the portrait were the words,

"I have done this for you; what have you done for me?"

Zinzendorf stood motionless in front of the painting, watching his Savior suffer and bleed, and said to himself, "I have loved Him for a long time, but I have never actually done anything for Him. From now on I will do whatever He leads me to do."

For the rest of his life, Zinzendorf considered this encounter a turning point. The blood of Jesus had a central place in his life and in the ministry of the Moravians.

The story is told that when the first two young Moravian missionaries boarded the ship in Copenhagen to sail to the West Indies, perhaps never to return (as 20 out of the first 29 missionaries died in those first years), they lifted their hands and cried out to their friends on shore:

"May the Lamb that was slain receive the reward for His suffering!"

This became the rally cry of the Moravian missions movement. The Moravians knew that Jesus had purchased with the price of His own blood, souls from every nation, tribe, and tongue (Revelation 5:9-10), and it propelled them to action.

"And they sang a new song, saying, 'Worthy are you to take the scroll and to open its seals, for you were slain, and by your blood you ransomed people for God from every tribe and language and people and nation, and you have made them a kingdom and priests to our God, and they shall reign on the earth.'"

Notice how the Lamb of God is worshiped in this passage: Jesus has ransomed, with His precious blood, persons from every people group in the world—every tribe, every culture, every language group. The reward of His suffering is the gathering in of worshipers from all the peoples of the world. We must remember that the blood of Jesus was shed not just to purchase us, but the worldwide Church of God from all nations.

## REMEMBERING THE NATIONS AT THE LORD'S SUPPER

Once I was participating in a retreat near Philadelphia with a church I had served as a missions coach. They had recently launched a church-wide vision which included a focus on the Tarahumara people of Central Mexico. After a moving service with an extended time of worship, we came to the Lord's Table together.

Pastor Gil Trusty, now one of my closest friends, kneeled down at the table, and after drawing attention to the remaining bread and wine, he prayed—tears streamed down his cheeks:

"Father, this is reserved for the Tarahumara people. It is a symbol for us, of the Tarahumara who don't yet eat and drink from this table, but they will, they will. Reservations have been made by Jesus but we must invite them to come. We must pursue what your Son bled to obtain. Father, may the Lamb that was slain receive His reward through our church, the worship of the Tarahumara."

This would forever change the way I approach the Lord's Supper. Now when I experience communion, I take notice of the remaining uneaten bread and the undrunk wine and remember the nations, the reward of His suffering.

As He says in John 10:16, "I have other sheep that are not of this fold. I must bring them also, and they will listen to my voice. So there will be one flock, one shepherd."

Why missions?

1. Because God's heart beats for the nations.

2. Because salvation is found only in Jesus.

3. Because our churches can't afford not to do missions.

4. Because we are called to know God and make Him known.

5. Because the Lamb deserves His reward.

Do these five foundational motives for missions offer us any clues about what to prioritize and how to pursue our global outreach efforts?

## chapter 4

# IS EVERY CHRISTIAN A MISSIONARY?

by Denny Spitters

*YOU ARE NOW ENTERING THE MISSION FIELD! –*
*Sign posted at church parking lot exit*

## ASSUMPTIONS AND IMPLICATIONS TO CONSIDER

NOT LONG AGO I participated in a conference of evangelical churches on the topic of how to be a strategic sending church. After a time of greeting and worship, one of the hosts stepped forward to outline the conference focus. His appeal was based on John 20:21, often rendered, "As the Father has sent me, so send I you." He framed the conference around his conviction that every believer is sent, therefore everybody in the church is a missionary. If all believers called themselves missionaries and learned to live and act like missionaries, and if this became the central focus of training in our churches, mission outreach would naturally unfold everywhere we went, local or global, without distinction.

Others at this event asserted that when a church calls certain people missionaries, the rest of the people in the church (who are also *missionaries*) are disenfranchised. They argued that this practice is one of the greatest reasons most believers are not bold enough to share their faith in their own context.

Some see this as a tension between the local church and the mission industry: the local church wants to embrace the sent-ness of its members, while missionaries and mission agencies try to protect their turf and status. That may be the case at times.

Yet are there clear biblical distinctions behind the role of a missionary? Or is it true that ultimately all of us are missionaries, whether we teach, preach, and plant churches in other countries, or serve as marketplace missionaries in our very own cities? The sign over many a church door or posted at the parking lot exit tells those who go out that they are now entering their mission fields. Is this kind of thinking true or helpful?

## LIVING AS SENT ONES

John 20:21 does indeed make clear that Jesus has sent us as the Father sent Him. The priesthood of all believers (1 Peter 2:5-9) comes with the empowerment and responsibility to declare the praises of Him who called us out of darkness into His wonderful light. In the Great Commission of Matthew 28:18-20, every follower of Christ is a disciple who is to make disciples; missionaries do not carry these imperatives as their exclusive privilege. You could say that every disciple is "on mission" for the proclamation of the gospel. Does that make everyone a missionary? Or are missionaries in any sense unique or set apart—as pastors and elders are?

> **Is it true that ultimately all of us are missionaries, whether we teach, preach, and plant churches in other countries, or serve as marketplace missionaries in our very own cities?**

As biblical scholars note, we must be careful to distinguish between God's commission to all Christians and that which He gives to the Church as a whole or to specific people. When Paul calls us the body of Christ, he points out that all parts are not the same (1 Corinthians 12:12-30). God seems to give people different gifts and callings. All Christians are to live generously, but not everyone has the gift of giving. Disciples of

Christ are to share the gospel with those around them, but not all have the gift of evangelism. All believers are to care for one another, but not all are to be pastors or elders.

## MISSIONS AND EVANGELISM

What do people mean when they say "all Christians are missionaries"? Let's take a closer look at some of the most quoted statements along these lines and what they speak to regarding missions.

- Charles Spurgeon: "Every Christian here is either a missionary or an impostor."[41] Very famous quote. Very influential preacher. However, does Spurgeon simply mean that the proof of a disciple of Christ is his genuine outreach to the world around him?

- Winkie Pratney: "Every Christian a missionary; every non-Christian a mission-field."[42] Is Pratney, a New Zealand evangelist and author, urging every Christian to take responsibility for living and speaking the gospel through evangelism to unbelievers, or something more?

- Count Ludwig Von Zinzendorf: "Missions, is simply this: Every heart with Christ is a missionary, every heart without Christ a mission field."[43] Is Zinzendorf, founder of the Moravian world missions movement, primarily making the point that evangelism is the central focus of cross-cultural missions, or is he saying that evangelism and mission are the same?

- Alan Hirsch: "Christians who earn a living as teachers, accountants, store clerks, mechanics, plumbers, doctors, whatever—you are a missionary!"[44] Is Hirsch claiming that believers should identify as missionaries no matter what they do vocationally, or stating that no matter our vocations, we should identify ourselves as "living sent" within that vocation?

Each statement expresses a passionate motivation for every disciple within the body of Christ to be propelled into vibrant, outward expressions of faith by word and deed. Sharing our faith is every disciple's responsibility. Each of them implores us to channel the outward flow of the gospel through our lives. With this we fully agree.

Each of these statements zeroes in on the responsibility of every believer to readily engage others in evangelism. But are sharing our faith and doing missions the same thing? Are missions and evangelism synonymous?

## ARE THEY THE SAME?

We assert that while evangelism is central to making disciples, and making disciples the core of our commission, missions is *not* the same as evangelism, and the choice to call all Christians missionaries or potential missionaries, though its intent may be to bestow a sense of purpose and motivation on more of us in the body of Christ, comes with a cost. It deprives us of language to describe those who are uniquely set apart to pioneer the gospel across the boundaries it has yet to cross. The expectation that encouraging every Christian to identify himself or herself as a missionary will produce the activity of greater outreach and evangelism has some significant flaws.

Justin Long compares these two terms well: "We say 'every member a missionary' but we don't actually mean it," he says. What we really mean is this:

- 'every member a witness' (ready to give testimony to what God has done in your life)

- 'every member an evangelist' (ready to share the Good News of salvation)

- 'every member a disciple maker' (who works deeply with people to help them grow in their obedience to Jesus).

68

"But 'missionary' means (a) sent (b) across a boundary to where the Gospel is not (c) to see a church planted (not just converts made) that (d) can reach everyone in that place without the missionary being present (through the work of witnesses, evangelists, pastors, etc.)."[45]

## A BIBLICAL FILTER

Can we find the word *missionary* used or defined in our Bibles? If it doesn't appear in the Bible, attempts to provide a "biblical" definition must have their limits. Yet to say *missionary* is an extra-biblical concept may also go too far. Kevin DeYoung claims,

"At the most basic level, *a missionary is someone who has been sent.* That's what the word 'mission' entails. It may not appear in your English Bibles, but it's still a biblical word."[46]

It seems clear the idea that certain individuals are set aside and sent out for missionary purposes does appear in Scripture (e.g., "Set apart for me Barnabas and Saul for the work to which I have called them" [Acts 13:2]).

The word *apostle* is used more than 80 times in the New Testament. It simply means a messenger or one who was sent to transmit a message. The New Testament also uses the term in a more narrow way to refer to the inner circle of Christ's disciples, including Paul who was given the title by Jesus Himself.

Please note we do *not* hold that the role or office of Apostle, in this latter sense, exists today. We use the term in the sense it is used in Ephesians 4:11-13, as the role of those equipping the people of God for the works of service and ministry. They are gifted with the role of the advancement of the gospel where it is yet unknown. Apostles may also have a unique, entrepreneurial role in pioneering this leading edge of gospel revelation, as Paul describes in Romans 15:20-21 (NASB):

"And thus I aspired to preach the gospel, not where Christ was already named, so that I would not build on another man's foundation; but as it is written,

'They who had no news of Him shall see,
And they who have not heard shall understand.'"

We also find it helpful to connect the term *apostle* with the word *ambassador*, which means an authorized messenger or representative (e.g., in 2 Corinthians 5:20). Ambassadors were and are sent as emissaries on missions representing those who send them and have often faced unknown and hostile environments. They were to consider themselves expendable, rather than expecting a royal treatment some ambassadors can expect today. The use of the word *apostle* to mean a messenger or ambassador has been lost today except in cases where the term is translated into Latin with the word *missio*, from which we get the word *missionary*, so we can reasonably describe missionaries as having an apostolic function.

> A missionary, like an apostle, may be seen as an ambassador sent on a mission for the King.

A missionary, like an apostle, may be seen as an ambassador sent on a mission for the King. This does not suggest a special rank, but a unique role. Apostolic missionaries are not superstar Christians, but they are called and gifted by God to be sent out for the crossing of barriers to bring the message of the gospel and make disciples of the nations.

In much the same way a teaching elder or pastor needs certain God-given gifts and qualifications for the ministry of teaching, apostolic missionaries need to possess certain skills and God-given abilities recognized by those who commission them. John encourages the support of such workers (3 John 6-8):

"You will do well to send them on their journey in a manner worthy of God. For they have gone out for the sake of the name, accepting nothing from the Gentiles. Therefore we ought to support people like these, that we may be fellow workers for the truth."

We note that although this passage "sets apart" these apostolic missionaries for specific service, it clearly commends participation in the mission by other followers of Christ. Everyone has a part to play. The mission does not belong solely to missionaries. Missionaries who behave as if it does are on thin ice, as we will explore in the next chapter.

## MORE NARROW DEFINITIONS

A more narrow use of the term "missionary," one that offers clarity and definition, describes missionaries as those who are sent to plant the gospel within a target culture until it expands throughout that culture and perhaps beyond. It may not be possible to give a flawless definition of a missionary, nor one on which we can all agree, but this does not excuse having no definition at all. Missiologist Herbert Kane suggests the following:

"In the traditional sense the term missionary has been reserved for those who have been called by God to a full-time ministry of the Word and prayer (Acts 6:4), and who have crossed geographical and/or cultural boundaries (Acts 22:21) to preach the gospel in those areas of the world where Jesus Christ is largely, if not entirely unknown (Romans 15:20). This definition, though by no means perfect, has the virtue of being Biblical."[47]

Again, this does not make those who serve in such roles better or more important to others in the body of Christ. In fact, putting current or past missionaries on a pedestal or describing them as heroes (as some well-meaning mission mobilizers and recruiters may tend to do) can be a big problem. Holding up missionaries as an exclusive and holier class may send the false message that the rest of us in the Church are second-class Christians who pay these professionals to carry out our mission by proxy. All Christians are called to participate in the Great Commission—globally as well as locally, we would say. All are included in God's global mission. But not all Christians are called to be apostolic missionaries.

## CALLED AND GIFTED

In the context of missions and ministry, the words *call* and *calling* may elicit varying degrees of anxiety, confusion, and confidence. It is first essential to separate the *general call* of Scripture with its commands and direction for the whole church from the more specific, *individual calling* many rely on to find their place vocationally and/or in ministry.

It seems clear that a believer's specific sense of calling should be rooted in the context of the teachings of Scripture and the structure of the local church, which is to identify, affirm, confirm, and send out workers (as we see in Acts 13). Yet we see the words "God has called me" too often used to end a conversation with the church rather than to begin one, circumventing any testing of character, preparation, or clarifying of calling—as if God's direction can only be known by the individual or family that has been "called."

Missionary candidates need more than a calling; they also need gifts that align with their ministry. The ultimate purpose of those gifts is to help make disciples. As Os Guiness reminds us,

"In the biblical understanding of giftedness, gifts are never really ours or for ourselves. We have nothing that was not given us. Our gifts are ultimately God's, and we are only 'stewards'—responsible for the prudent management of property that is not our own. This is why our gifts are always 'ours for others,' whether in the community of Christ or the broader society outside, especially the neighbor in need.

"This is also why it is wrong to treat God as a grand employment agency, a celestial executive searcher to find perfect fits for our perfect gifts. The truth is not that God is finding us a place for our gifts but that God has created us and our gifts for a place of his choosing—and we will only be ourselves when we are finally there."[48]

## MISSIONARY: REPLACE OR RECLAIM?

Brian D. McLaren, a writer of influence within the emerging church movement, is one of those who proclaims without reservation that "every Christian is a missionary and every place is a mission field."[49]

Interacting with this statement in an article for *Evangelical Missions Quarterly,* pastor Greg Wilton points out that it can "distort the specific calling on some Christians to devote their lives to full-time, cross-cultural witness," and this is our concern as well. Wilton quotes missiologists Steven Strauss and Craig Ott who say (much as Stephen Neill said years before),

> **If we choose to call every Christian a missionary, then we will need to create a new term for the Christian who is specially called, gifted, and commissioned for cross-cultural mission.**

"If we nevertheless choose to call every Christian a missionary, then we will need to create a new term for the Christian who is specially called, gifted, and commissioned for cross-cultural mission. Otherwise, this unique, essential, and divinely appointed role is at risk of being lost altogether."[50]

Wilton explains:

"Strauss and Ott believe that all Christians are called to live on mission for God, but some are called to mission in a specific way. They believe the word 'missionary' was created to help define a particular group of Christian men and women who were called to fill a particular kind of mission.

"McLaren's position and Strauss and Ott's position are reflective of two sides of the coin. While both sides may agree that all Christians are called and commanded to obey Jesus' Great Commission, they disagree about the distinct identification of a missionary."[51]

What does Wilton conclude?

"Am I really a missionary? Should that also be said of us? Are we all missionaries? My direct and simple answer to this question is 'no.'... *The word is too precious and vital to what God in his sovereign plan intends to do throughout the world.*"[52]

## WORDS WITH BAGGAGE

Some reject or define the words mission and missionary because they see them as too narrow or exclusive. Others reject them because, in English, they offer some linguistic challenges. And many, perhaps, would put these words behind us due to negative associations.

The motivation to reject words that have acquired negative or confusing connotations is understandable. I vividly remember a discussion with a close friend when I decided to disassociate myself from the word *Christian*. There are too many negatives and hurdles within our culture to overcome, I pointed out. Asked if I was a Christian, I would quickly deny it and identify myself instead as "a follower of Jesus."

After a pregnant pause, my friend replied, "Brother, for over 2,000 years *Christians* is what your 'followers of Jesus' have been called, and that includes all the good, the bad, and the ugly. It is the defining word of who we are. Own it! Denial and reframing usually only bring confusion and further uncertainty. Don't presume you can extract yourself from the disinformation, potential ridicule, or rejection—or its historicity for that matter. Embrace it! It's who we are!"

Similarly, attempts to replace the term *missionary* due to unpleasant or misleading associations have done as much to create confusion as to dispel it. The general tenor and thrust of Scripture gives ample support for use of the term *missionary*. This word is not essential, but some kind of language and clarity is, even if exact precision is not possible.

We don't reject creative language or the use of terms such as cross-cultural worker, kingdom worker, and tentmaker. Certainly, we recognize that those serving in hostile environments may find it wise and necessary to avoid being openly known as missionaries. But we also believe it is time for the Church to recover, reclaim, and restore the amazing God-inspired *role* of the apostolic, cross-cultural missionary for the sake of God's kingdom purposes and for the soul of the Church.

This may be a good time to note that though I serve with a mission agency, I do not consider myself a missionary. The primary function of ministries or agencies that in a myriad of ways assist churches in sending out missionaries is mobilization. To our view, this role is vital to the process of sending. It often requires working in full-time ministry and raising support. Mission agency staff and other mobilizers are worthy of the Church's support and encouragement. But we do not believe that a biblical understanding of the missionary task requires that they be identified as missionaries.

## MISSIONARY AS COLONIALIST

It may be helpful to address some of the negative associations with missionary language more directly. Words like *missions* and *missionary* may seem colonial, arrogant, controversial, violent, outdated, or pejorative.

At times I'm asked about my role at Pioneers. When I reply that I mobilize, encourage, and help churches to send missionaries to unreached people groups where there are no disciples or churches, some look at me with wide-eyed horror. They may ask, "You don't really mean sending missionaries, do you? Is that even needed or done anymore?"

These objections may be rooted in a narrative put forward in our society and taught in our schools that missionaries have historically and directly contributed to the exploitation, destruction, and dominance of other cultures. While missions history has some dark moments, to attribute the abuses of colonialism to missionaries is to suggest guilt by association.

**Many in our congregations are ignorant of the great contributions missionaries have made to better societies and to fight injustice, rather than to propagate it.**

It should be noted that church mission leaders may not hold such critical views of mission history, though some do. Our experience suggests that many in our congregations are ignorant of the great contributions missionaries have made to better societies and to fight injustice, rather than to propagate it. Far from being colonial in their thinking, many missionaries have taken a stand against such exploitation and fought to bring it to an end.

Sociologist Robert D. Woodberry has done extensive research on this and related questions.

"'We don't have to deny that there were and are racist missionaries,' says Woodberry. 'We don't have to deny there were and are missionaries who do self-centered things. But if that were the average effect, we would expect the places where missionaries had influence to be worse than places where missionaries weren't allowed or were restricted in action. We find exactly the opposite on all kinds of outcomes.

Even in places where few people converted; [missionaries] had a profound economic and political impact.'"[53]

After years of analyzing statistical data and historical analyses and funded by a $500,000 grant with over 50 researchers combing through data, Woodberry could now support a sweeping claim linking gospel proclamation and social transformation:

"Areas where Protestant missionaries had a significant presence in the past are on average more economically developed today, with comparatively better health, lower infant mortality, lower corruption, greater literacy, higher educational attainment (especially for women), and more robust membership in nongovernmental associations."[54]

Woodberry's work has revealed the opposite of the narrative put forth that missionary work has primarily been destructive. He highlights the strong correlation between the intentional ministry of evangelism and discipleship these missionaries pursued and the fruit of it, which included significant social justice and transformation. Should we be surprised that missionaries who focused on personal gospel "conversion" from false religions to the Christ who "makes all things new" achieved great social and cultural advancement even without social and cultural change as their primary focus and motivation for service?

The gospel can transform cultures to become their *best*. When will we realize the rich heritage missionaries left as they planted the gospel among the unreached and the transformation of societies that resulted? Woodberry's research is just the tip of the iceberg. Maybe we have less reason to distance ourselves from previous mission efforts than we've been taught.

## A CATHOLIC MISSIONS PARALLEL

How has the concept that "every Christian is a missionary and every ministry of the church is missions" affected other institutions of religion which have adopted it?

Robert Royal, who manages an online Catholic forum, connects a broadening definition of missions with the death of missions within the Catholic Church:

"Not that long ago, when you talked about the death of missionaries, it meant that they had met some sad end in a far-flung corner of the world. More recently, it means that no one much feels the need to 'preach the Gospel to all nations' anymore—and that missionary work is essentially disappearing. Our modern Gospel is much simpler: We're all basically good people already, aren't we? So why can't we respect and affirm one another's lifestyles, and all just try and get along.

"...That seems to be the default setting now, even for many Christians...

"... the whole spirit of missionary work is drying up. Long gone are the days when Catholic children fasted during Lent and sent in their mite boxes for the missions—a sign that the adults aren't that serious about missions either."

Royal cites a Catholic mission leader who attributes these trends to the diffusion of missionary responsibility in the 1950s and 1960s, when it began to be said that the whole church is "missionary."

"It's an old but true maxim that what's everybody's responsibility is nobody's. How does 'the whole Church' reach out to distant peoples without proper institutions and an attitude that it must? The results, beyond all question, confirm that it can't."

In addition, he reports, many embraced concrete secular projects that people could agree on and feel good about. Many presumed these more accessible efforts would lead to an increase in those who recognized a "vocation" (calling) to missions.

"They didn't ... Today, our missionaries engage in national campaigns about foreign debt, against arms production, against counterfeited medications, and for public water access: today, one no longer speaks of missions to the nations, but of worldliness and of social or ecological efforts. Can you tell me how many young men or women get enthusiastic or become missionaries after a demonstration protesting arms production? None."[55]

Will evangelical Protestants make the same mistakes, disbanding mission structures without replacing them and embracing secular values while rejecting biblical distinctives and the centrality of the gospel? Will mission, for us, become everything but making disciples of the nations?

## WHAT HAPPENS WHEN WE STRETCH A PARADIGM TOO FAR?

Voices promoting the "every Christian a missionary" message have projected a result of greater evangelism, discipleship, and outreach—including more getting a taste of cross-cultural ministry and pursuing long-term, full-time service. But this has not been the case. To our knowledge no research has been attempted that would prove/disprove a direct correlation to increased cross-cultural service. Our experience and anecdotal observation of the last several decades reveals scant evidence of missional progression leading to increased cross-cultural service. We can see the parallel to this with the dramatic explosion of short-term missions trips in the 1980s and 1990s which failed to produce the dramatic increase in new long-term workers that many predicted.[56] At best, cross-cultural mission sending has stayed the same, and in specific contexts, churches shut down or pull away from cross-cultural mission efforts in favor of other pursuits.

Could it be that when too many are told to assume a role that they are neither equipped nor called to pursue, the result is a church where missions is impaired, impoverished, and weakened?

Broad definitions of "who is a missionary" may also create a kind of "tone-deafness" among church leaders, preventing them from recognizing and equipping those God is calling into apostolic missionary roles: "Well, John, that's great that you sense God speaking to you about cross-cultural missions, but you know—all of us are missionaries!"

Postmodern thinking, faulty perspectives on the biblical basis and history of missions, and a culture of individualism seem to have so influenced the North American Church that distinctions about ministry roles and goals no longer matter.

When we stretch the definition of missions and missionaries too far, missions in any traditional sense is marginalized. We believe this will only be remedied when the entire body of Christ is focused on Great Commission obedience that includes the thrusting out of workers to the ends of the earth.

It is not too late for the North American church to reassert that missionaries are sent-out ones—to cast aside the notion that everything is missions and everybody is a missionary, or that the debate is only a semantic one. We believe the future health of the Church and the advancement of the gospel in our own context is directly linked to thinking clearly about the mission task and missionary roles.

**When we stretch the definition of missions and missionaries too far, missions in any traditional sense is marginalized.**

To go and make disciples of all nations and send out those whom God has called for specific purposes is not only a command, it is the very lifeblood of our task—of advancing the gospel and joining in the work of Jesus to build His global Church.

## chapter 5

# HOW ARE MISSIONARIES SENT?

by Denny Spitters

*How then will they call on him in whom they have not believed? And how will they believe in him of whom they have never heard? And how are they to hear without someone preaching? And how are they to preach unless they are sent? Just as it is written, "How beautiful are the feet of those who preach the good news!" — Romans 10:14-15*

## THE ESSENTIAL ROLE OF THE LOCAL CHURCH

THE TELEVISION SERIES *Travel the Road* premiered in 2003 with a goal of capturing "the raw and authentic stories of missionaries Timothy Scott and William Decker, as they set out on Gospel Expeditions to the most remote and unreached lands of the world."[57]

We love Tim and Will's spirit of obedience. Just go! Their vision is to go to the hardest and most remote places and where the gospel may not have been preached. It makes for a highly compelling reality TV adventure.

On the other hand, Timothy and William also freely admit Will was not a believer when they started in 2003 (though he has since become one). And, though they've raised up an audience of followers and have the accountability of the camera lens, we do not observe that any church fellowship affirmed, confirmed, or sent them.

Their approach to ministry also has some significant weaknesses. Though they show sacrifice and boldness in in their commitment to go and preach the gospel—usually through a translator—they seem to quickly move on to the next location for another episode, seeming to leaving those who respond to their message fend for themselves. In contrast with the example of Acts 14:21-23, we see no signs that they are making disciples or working to establish a church within the contexts they visit.

Some of these weaknesses may come with the medium. Seeking out ever-more-compelling episodes and new remote locations, television may elevate and oversimplify their ministry, placing Timothy and William (however good their intentions might be) at the center of missions activity without either the support of a local church at home or the birth of local churches in their location. But how does discipleship, either for Tim and Will or for those they may reach, happen with such an approach? Can new believers blossom and grow without the fellowship of a church family?

**The New Testament model of gospel proclamation exemplified by Paul, Barnabas, and others always involved intentional discipleship and the establishment of those believers into local churches.**

Consider the contrasting picture painted by Kevin DeYoung and Greg Gilbert in their book *What Is the Mission of the Church?*

"The mission of the church is to go into the world and make disciples by declaring the gospel of Jesus Christ in the power of the Spirit and gathering these disciples into churches, that they might worship and obey Jesus Christ now and in eternity to the glory of God the Father."[58]

Though an emphasis on evangelism and conversion-counting may be seem normal to many American Christians today, the New Testament model of gospel proclamation exemplified by Paul, Barnabas, and others always involved intentional discipleship and the establishment of those believers into local churches. Do some of today's models leave out these key aspects?

## THE SENT AND SENDER RELATIONSHIP

This brings us to the question of calling. If God calls, equips, and gifts some people to cross barriers of language, culture, and geography to make disciples, how do we know that? Is it primarily a "you and God" process, where we hear from God about where He wants us to go, then share the news with others so they can partner with us to provide the resources needed?

I am amazed at the abundance of ministries whose websites emphasize finding and pursuing our mission callings with little mention of the local church. It's as if the church is not part of the process, or if it is, plays only a superfluous, rubber-stamping role. Most of these organizations have good vision statements and some mention partnering with local churches on the field. But where is the local church on the front end? Can or should local churches have a foundational role in the process of sending?

If missionaries are sent-ones, they don't just go to the lost and unreached, they are sent to the lost and unreached. Who sends them? Is it just between them and God? Or them and God and a mission agency? In North America, we often see either individuals, agencies, or both considered the foundation of the sending process. But the book of Acts paints a different picture.

We hold to the conviction that Acts is not a merely a historical descriptive account, but a writing inspired by the Holy Spirit with prescriptive intent: It is written to teach us and to provide models for us to follow. Acts 13:1-4 provides a clear pattern for the sending process, and the local church is at the very center:

"Now there were in the church at Antioch prophets and teachers, Barnabas, Simeon who was called Niger, Lucius of Cyrene, Manaen a lifelong friend of Herod the tetrarch, and Saul. While they were worshiping the Lord and fasting, the Holy Spirit said, 'Set apart for me Barnabas and Saul for the work to which I have called them.' Then after fasting and praying they laid their hands on them and sent them off.

"So, being sent out by the Holy Spirit, they went down to Seleucia, and from there they sailed to Cyprus."

Note the points of connection between God, the local church, and their missionary team (missionaries):

- The leaders' worship, prayer, and fasting brings recognition of God's designed mission and timing.
- The Holy Spirit identifies an apostolic team (Saul and Barnabas) from the church who are set apart for the work..
- The mission team sent out by the Holy Spirit and released by the church.
- A process of confirmation revealed the previous preparation of the team and the church.
- The team was affirmed, commissioned, and released through the praying and laying on of hands by the church.
- The church embraced the privilege of sending, commending, and releasing qualified team members.
- The missionaries were not Lone Rangers; partnership was central to the process.

## CHURCH-BASED SENDING OR PERSONAL CALL?

When highly individualistic North Americans seek support for their mission efforts from a local church, they often put their vision at the center and ask for churches to get on board by providing resources. This approach, however, can short-circuit the partnering process God designed to benefit both the missionary and the local church.

A recent book gives a clear example of this from today's church culture:

"What is the relationship between an individual's 'missionary call' and the local church? Several years ago, I was asked to make contact with a young man to explain to him how we, at our church, practiced missions. He wanted to aggressively pursue cross-cultural ministry overseas. There weren't many men advising him at the time, and he was about to make some very important decisions about missionary service. In our phone conversation, I asked what his church thought about his very detailed plan for the future, since he seemed to have everything figured out. He was puzzled and quickly informed me that guidance for his future was essentially up to him and the Holy Spirit. When I respectfully disagreed, he firmly stated that it was all about him and the Holy Spirit—and no one else. He explained that he answered to God alone. It was a very American response."[59]

The paradigm we see in Acts 13 shows local church leadership recognizing and affirming a call and released the missionaries to the work. The Holy Spirit spoke to both the team and the church leadership to bring clarity and unity.

## A MISSION FOR US, NOT ME

One central reason for a highly individualized view of mission may be our tendency, in studying the Bible, to read "you" as singular in context rather than plural. Some scholars say "you" in the biblical canon is plural at least 98% of the time. At least 4,720 verses (2,698 in the Hebrew Bible and 2,022 in the Greek New Testament) include a plural "you" which may be lost in translation into English. We easily read and interpret instructions as if they are directed to us personally rather than the Church as a community. No wonder we find false reinforcement for poor thinking about missions or even our own discipleship—it's all about me. What if responding to God's call and obeying His commands was something we did together as a community rather than something we expected to carry out as individuals? Would our approach to going and sending change?

We believe missionary sending is meant to be carried out in partnership with the local community of faith, working together to prepare, train, assess, and confirm believers for the work to which God has called them. Part of this sending process includes testing a calling, since, as experience suggests, not everyone who wants to be sent as a missionary *should* be sent as a missionary.

## LOCAL CHURCH AS MOBILIZER

The local church, if obedient and willing, is central and vital to this process of mobilization, preparation, and sending. When the church is not willing, those looking to pursue a potential missionary call usually become frustrated and discouraged. Yet in Acts we see a vibrant, outward focused, Holy-Spirit-led church that recognized the qualities and calling of a team God had brought together right before their eyes and they were prepared to listen and act. What a contrast.

> We believe missionary sending is meant to be carried out in partnership with the local community of faith, working together to prepare, train, assess and confirm believers for the work to which God has called them.

How important and central should the local church be in the mobilization process? In the introduction to his book *Missions Smart,* David Frazier asks who is responsible for the gaps in the missionary preparation that can often result in preventable missionary attrition. Is it mission agencies with their expertise in training, member care, and field leadership? Seminaries and training institutions? Local sending churches? He concludes,

"If cross-cultural workers need certain qualities to be effective and resilient, once again, the heavy responsibility for development and selection falls on candidates and their home sending churches, not on agencies or training centers.

"...Local churches and candidates must take a serious look at the present statistics of missionary attrition and be careful not to assume that agencies or training courses can do all that is needed to screen, counsel, and test candidates. By saying 'We are not mission agencies,' churches are giving organizations responsibilities they were never designed or equipped to handle."[60]

"...To summarize, no theological school, cross-cultural training institute, expert agency training system, ideal team environment, or well-staffed member-care group can make someone thrive and be effective overseas if their character, giftings, and skills have not already been developed, tested and proven over time in a home church and local international community."[61]

We agree with Frazier. The home or sending church and the community are to play a crucial role in the identification and confirmation of missionaries and pursuit of viable cross-cultural ministry. The partnership between the candidates and the sending church described in Acts 13:1-4 is brief but sufficient to provide an accurate and adequately defined process for a robust sending relationship.

Christians tend to think Paul met Jesus on the road to Damascus and a year or two later got sent out from Antioch on his first missionary journey, but it was actually many years. We forget or fail to observe his long season of preparation. Paul spent time in Arabia, Damascus, Jerusalem, Syria, and Cilicia before revisiting Jerusalem years later. Acts 11:25-26 says,

"So Barnabas went to Tarsus to look for Saul, and when he found him, he brought him to Antioch. For a whole year they met with the church and taught a great many people. And in Antioch the disciples were first called Christians."

Antioch would be the sending church for all three of Paul's missionary journeys, beginning with the one recorded in Acts 13:1-4. This church recognized and knew the vision of this team. So it was no surprise when the Holy Spirit said, "set them apart for the work to which I called them." A missionary's ministry flows from a community of faith with a compelling missions vision—a community where they are *known*.

## HEALTHY PARTNERSHIPS BETWEEN CHURCHES AND MINISTRIES

In his book *A Biblical Theology of Missions,* George Peters points out that mission history is often written to emphasize great personalities and mission societies; only in unusual cases does it tell the story of the Church. As a result, many perceive missions as the responsibility of individuals rather than the mandate of the church. He caps this observation with a strong warning that this misperception has produced "autonomous, missionless churches on one hand and autonomous churchless societies on the other hand." [62]

So what part does each play in the advance of the glory of God to the nations? Pastor Steve Beirn spells it out plainly in *Well Sent:*

"The church is to be the sender of missionaries, and the agency is to be the facilitator. The church has most (but not all) of the resources, and the agency has most (but not all) of the expertise. It makes sense to bring these parties together for productive ministry. It is important to know that 'going it alone' often results in a duplication of efforts and a lack of expertise.

"When attempting to bring the church and the agency together, it is important to understand their intended roles. An inadequate view of the church's place in missions will diminish its sense of ownership and will create an inaccurate partnership with the agency."[63]

Healthy partnership between churches and agencies can go a long way to fostering Great Commission ministry. Churches that attempt to function without a partnership are often influenced by what they see as agency processes that are bulky or burdensome. Agencies also need to wake up to the reality that their structures need to be more decentralized and flexible to accommodate the churches who seek greater ownership and engagement in the sending process.

We recommend that churches and agencies establish a relationship of partnership and trust based on alignment in the following areas:

- Vision, core values, and ministry paradigms: How do we align and where do we differ?

- Expectations and responsibilities: Who does what and when? Who has the best capacity, capability, and expertise in a missionary's timeline from confirmation to field service?

- Communication: How will it be regular and clear and what systems will be used?

- Member care: How will both engage to best care for workers?

- Risk management: How will crises be handled and what protocols will be in place for the workers care?

- Finances and funding: What are the costs for deployment, field support, and ministry funding for workers?

- Accountability: How will the church, missionary, and agency maintain healthy mutual accountability?

When local churches, regardless of size or capacity, embrace an intentional vision of discipleship that promotes the affirmation and confirmation of those whom the Holy Spirit is raising up to be sent ones while they engage with trustworthy partners to help facilitate that vision, both agencies and churches can discover the joy of making disciples of all nations and experience what it means to be "blessed to be a blessing."

## chapter 6
# SO WHAT?

by Matthew Ellison

*The danger is that with the discussion about "being missional" and "every Christian being a missionary," the pursuit of all the peoples by prioritizing the unreached can be obscured. — David Mathis*

*After this I looked, and behold, a great multitude that no one could number, from every nation, from all tribes and peoples and languages... — Revelation 7:9*

## CONSIDERING WHAT IS AT STAKE

In 2015, DENNY AND I were a part of launching *The Mission Table,* a web-based, interactive missions conversation—basically an internet colloquium where leading missions thinkers and practitioners would tackle some of most the critical and controversial topics impacting global evangelization today.

We had been talking for a few years about reasons churches weren't doing missions well and felt that one of the primary ones was because they were not thinking about missions well. The tag line of *The Mission Table,* "Moving Conversation," is a double entendre; the aim is to help move conversations about missions to new levels. We hope these conversations will move God's people to think biblically and critically about missions.

You might say that The Mission Table places poor thinking about missions in its crosshairs. The inaugural episode, "Everyone Is a Missionary," set the stage in this way:

"Missions has traditionally consisted of international or cross-cultural ministry for spiritual purposes. But today in many churches, missions has come to include outreach ministries that are within our own community and culture and are often social or economic in nature. This broadening definition of missions has inevitably led to a philosophy that says that every follower of Christ is a missionary.

"In this episode of *The Mission Table* we will explore the implications of this philosophy. Is it biblical? Is it helpful? Does it lead to more missions work being accomplished or less?"[64]

I sent a link of this episode to a good friend of mine who has been engaged in missions for over 20 years. When I asked him what he thought, he explained that he stopped watching halfway through the episode, concluding that the conversation, even though robust, was just semantics. I took his response to mean that our conversation was not fundamental, that he thought we were spinning our wheels talking about the meaning of *missions* and *missionary*, and that the real-world implications of such a conversation were of little consequence.

I disagreed completely. I believe that how we understand *missions* and subsequently *missionary* are fundamental issues that have unbelievably significant consequences in life and eternity.

So, what's the big deal about calling every good, evangelistic or altruistic work a missions work? Must our gospel work be cross-cultural to be considered missions? And what's the harm in calling every follower of Christ a missionary? In this chapter we'll explore several disturbing examples of what can result from today's thinking about what makes something missions.

## MERCENARY MISSIONARIES

When the largest and most prominent "native missionary" organization, Gospel for Asia, became embroiled in a financial scandal,[65] church leaders began asking me what happened. What went wrong? Should we still support this ministry? I noticed that people were quick to simply chalk up the debacle to corruption or "sin in the camp." Although that was certainly part of the problem, I believe that one of the most significant factors was actually faulty missiology. Poor thinking about missions led to problematic results.

Reflecting back on a previous chapter, remember that although the word *missionary* doesn't appear in the Bible, a description of the role does. The term *missionary* is closely linked to *apostle*, and an apostle is one who is sent out.

Think about this for just a moment. Is it even possible for someone to be a native missionary when being native implies being indigenous or local?

Let me be clear that we fully support the validity of indigenous ministries that honor Jesus and seek to expand the church within their culture. When, however, we call them native missionaries and believe they are crossing cultural boundaries with the gospel, we may be mistaken. And, if we think that investing a few dollars a month to support a national Christian means we're doing the best we can for the Great Commission, maybe we should take a closer look.

> If we think that that investing a few dollars a month to support a national Christian means we're doing the best we can for the Great Commission, maybe we should take a closer look.

Among the many half-truths that have deceived the Church is the myth of the "$40,000-a-year American missionary," a claim that it often costs thirty or forty times more to support a Western missionary as it would to fund a native missionary to do the same work.[66] This argument has been used to sway donors to back native missionaries since they were simply more cost efficient.

Bob Finley of Christian Aid Mission made a similar appeal but took it further, arguing that there was no biblical case for sending foreign, cross-cultural missionaries at all; foreign missionaries were harmful, colonial, and should be withdrawn in favor of supporting indigenous workers only. Finley makes the financial case this way:

> "It makes no sense to spend $60,000 of God's money annually sending an American with his family to live as a missionary in a poor country where hundreds of local citizens have been called of God to reach their own people, and have no personal support. Any one of them, already knowing the local languages, would be ten times more effective than the foreigner. And is likely to be eager to serve with support of $600 or less annually, because he lives on the same economic level as those being reached with the gospel. In many countries the support package of one American could supply the support and ministry needs of 50 native missionaries."[67]

Massive numbers of Christians redirected their giving away from the "more expensive and less effective" Western workers to the most cost-effective native missionaries.

What donors were not told was that many of these so-called native missionaries were *not* missionaries, sent-out ones, at all, rather they were local workers; more precisely they were local pastors subsidized to work among their own (reached) peoples. Native missionaries were not, in many cases, breaking new ground for the spread of the gospel among India's thousands of unreached people groups as the literature suggested.

And here's something that should concern us: An unprecedented number of churches in the West were convinced that they could obey the Great Commission by sending money to non-Western workers who could deliver the good news on the cheap aboard their bicycles. In the end, we believe that Western Christians' desires were manipulated to buy missions "on sale" and write checks rather than send their own sons and daughters; the multi-million-dollar native missionary empire was born.

## THE CASUALTIES OF A PROXY WAR

The number of missionaries that the West is sending to the mission field has been in decline for several years. The native missionary movement may be a cause as well as a result of this. Among the many reasons for a decline in western missionary sending may simply be that we have hired others to fight a war which God has also called us to fight. We will stay home and send money, like wealthy men hiring proxy soldiers to fight on their behalf. Don't get me wrong; I'm all for international partnerships—but not for outsourcing missions.

My late friend and mentor Robertson McQuilkin used to say, "God never called us to send others in our place. He called us to go!" I am coming to believe that when we sponsor proxy soldiers to advance the global cause of our King, we forfeit one of the highest privileges of following Christ and we ourselves are among the casualties. No local church should miss out on the encouragement and nourishment that will come to it by sending its best people.

## HOW DID WE GET HERE?

I contend that one of the key misunderstandings that brought us to this point is the teaching that every follower of Christ is a missionary. Poor missions thinking led us to poor missions practice. If everyone is a missionary, then local Christians ministering to their own communities, overseas, are missionaries. In fact, you're a native missionary, I'm a native missionary—absolutely every follower of Christ is a native missionary.

Are national Christians serving among their own people essential to God's kingdom purposes? Absolutely. An essential component needed to complete the back-breaking, darkness penetrating task of making disciples of all nations, by God's design, are missionaries: sent-out ones, as the saying now goes "from all nations to all nations." We should not embrace the one and neglect the other. To rely only on local witnesses to reach the nations is to do missions by proxy.

## MISSIONAL MISAPPROPRIATION

In much the same way, our local outreach and the way we think about it has sometimes had a dampening effect on our commitment to sending out missionaries. In the book *Finish the Mission,* Desiring God editor David Mathis describes both the promise and potential danger of the missional movement and how it came to be.

"The most insightful of those using the term recognize that the West is quickly becoming post-Christian and the shift raises important questions about what it means to do domestic ministry. Europe and North America have become more and more like a mission field—but a post-Christian, rather than a pre-Christian, field. Since the term *evangelism* carries for some the baggage (and narrowness) of Christendom days when the general biblical worldview was prevalent enough in society that street corner confrontations and stadium crusades found more traction and produced more genuine converts, the emergence of the term *missional* (somewhat in place of evangelistic) signifies that the times are changing in some significant degree, calling for new missions-like engagement and evangelistic holism. This fresh thinking is a good development, but with it comes a danger.

"The danger is that with the discussion about being *missional* and *every Christian being a missionary,* the pursuit of all the peoples by prioritizing the unreached can be obscured... The biblical theme is not merely that God reaches as many people as possible, but all the peoples. He intends to create worshipers of His Son from every tribe, tongue, and nations. The push for being missional captures something very important in the heart of God, but this is dangerous when it comes at the cost of something else essential in the heart of God: pursuing all the nations, not merely those who share our language and culture."[68]

Mathis points out that a missional philosophy that calls everything missions and every Christian a missionary obscures the biblical priority of reaching the unreached.

## SHOW ME THE MONEY

Now-shuttered Mars Hill megachurch in Seattle was not only a leading church in the missional movement, it was in fact a pioneer and proponent of the modern missional approach to ministry. Though they supported cross-cultural missions, they embraced a missional philosophy that purposefully softened the distinctions between evangelism and missions. It's no surprise then that millions of dollars in donations solicited for global, international missions mostly stayed at home.

Former church members filed a lawsuit complaining that they and thousands of other individuals who tithed at Mars Hill were allegedly defrauded by ex-pastor Mark Driscoll and general manager and then-executive elder John Sutton Turner. They claim that Mars Hill leadership solicited donations for one purpose and used them for another:

"At issue are millions donated by church members who were told offerings went to missions in Ethiopia and India through the church's 'Global Fund.' In reality, those tithes appear to have stayed right at home. To 'woo new donors,' the complaints says, Driscoll 'intentionally deceived all potential donors by marketing Global Fund as a fund for international missions, when, in fact, they intended to use the majority of the donations for domestic expansion of MHC.'"[69]

The complaint cites an internal memo in which Mars Hill allegedly outlines the benefits of the Global Fund, from which a percentage would be designated for "highly visible, marketable projects."

According to the complaint, the memo states that,

"Besides the obvious gain of increased funding, for a relatively low cost (e.g. $10K/month), supporting a few missionaries and benevolence projects would serve to deflect criticism, increase goodwill, and create opportunities to influence and learn from other ministries."[70]

"Church leaders have previously apologized for the 'confusion' over the Global Fund, a repository that by 2014 was taking in a self-reported $300,000 a month, some $10 million total, according to the complaint. At the time the allegations over the funds surfaced, the leaders said they never meant to mislead the church's followers about where the money was going."[71]

Of course it is unethical to solicit donations for one purpose and to use them for another, but if a church has a missions definition that considers everything they do an extension of their missional purpose, can't missions donations be legitimately used for anything and everything? If you are a part of a church where everyone is a missionary and everything is missions, you may have little grounds to protest. If it's all missions, and everyone is a missionary, what is the objection?

## MUSHY MISSIONS

One of the arguments that we have heard that supports calling everyone a missionary is the idea that doing so will elevate the role and contribution of every believer, leading to a greater number of people and resources mobilized for God's purposes. But is this true? I contend that when we blend everything together it has the opposite effect. Once again, "what is everybody's job is nobody's job." The Chinese have a proverb that when two men own a horse, it will starve; when two men own a boat, it will leak. Diffusing missions responsibility and making everything missions does not tend to centralize the priority of taking the gospel to all nations—on the contrary, it marginalizes it.

## COLLEGE SCHOLARSHIPS AS MISSIONS

I once worked with a church that, prior to going through a missions coaching process, had a definition of missions that included everything, and I mean *everything*. Among many other things, their mission budget covered college scholarships for students attending their denomination's university. Of course, if a church wants to help raise up and train her young men and women for ministry, that's great. But consider the problems with calling that missions and taking it from the missions budget; how easily we might prioritize funding education for our churches' sons and daughters over needs that seem more remote and less rewarding.

This church now has a missions definition that delineates between what they call *domestic ministry* and *cross-cultural missions*. They have subsequently deepened their engagement both locally and globally.

Their missions pastor at the time of this transition said,

"I now understand missions to be primarily the work of establishing the church in cross-cultural settings where there is no church or it is not strong enough to reproduce, and ministry to be the work of growing and strengthening the church where it already exists. Both are crucial and I minimize neither, but they are not the same. If we make everything missions, we don't do our work well. This discovery has changed the way our church does missions and ministry."

## CHILDREN'S MINISTRY AS MISSIONS

A good friend of mine traveling for ministry in Portland, Oregon a couple of years ago ended up with time on his hands and visited a church in the city. What he experienced at this church is a prime example of the serious danger of calling everything missions.

The church was in the process of developing a focus on unreached people groups and even had a display celebrating that developing focus. During the announcements, the pastor of children's ministries stood up and said, "How many of you would like to take a short-term missions trip? Let me see a show of hands!"

After a time for response, he said, "We're going to sweeten the deal even more. You will be going to work among an unreached people group, and you don't even need a passport! Plus, the church is going to pay *all* your expenses for the trip!" It doesn't get any better than that, does it?

So, where is this unreached people group?

"They're right here, they are in our basement! We need your help in the children's ministry. Come join us and reach this unreached people group. See me and I'll share more details with you."

Children's ministry is high and holy work. In fact, it may be some of the most important work that takes place within a local church. Jesus has a special place in His heart for kids and we should as well. But can we call the children within an evangelical church in the US "unreached"? Many of these kids have Christian parents, and even those who don't still have opportunity to hear the gospel. Compare this with truly unreached children within truly unreached peoples with no impulse for children's ministry in Jesus' name, precisely because there are no witnessing gospel churches.

An unreached person is not someone in our churches who doesn't follow Christ. An unreached person is not even a neighbor who doesn't follow Christ and has never heard a clear presentation of the gospel (but could if we would simply cross the street). An unreached person is someone with no access the gospel and who could not hear it even if they wanted to.

By all means let us prioritize making disciples of our own children. If we consider this to be our part in discipling the nations, though, many of the world's children will be left out.

## CHRISTIAN RADIO IN THE US AS MISSIONS

One church I worked with several years ago celebrated the high percentage of their overall budget that was being given to missions. The lion's share of it was funding Christian radio ministry in the US. After clarifying a biblical definition of missions, they rightly concluded that the percentage they were truly giving to missions was far, far smaller than they had originally thought. When they realized that, they continued to support Christian radio but also began to increase their giving to take the gospel cross-culturally.

I see it as a major stretch to consider the funding of Christian radio in the US part of a church's global missions budget. In no way am I attacking Christian radio; I have often benefited from Christian radio and supported it. However, in my opinion even to consider it domestic evangelism and outreach is a stretch.

> By all means let us prioritize making disciples of our own children. If we consider this to be our part in discipling the nations, though, many of the world's children will be left out.

Though I realize that periodically unbelievers tune in and hear the gospel, let's be honest: Christian radio is mostly listened to by Christians. Let's not spend our mission money on what ministers primarily to ourselves.

## THE NUMBERS SPEAK

Still not convinced that calling every Christian a missionary and every outreach ministry *missions* is a fundamental issue, not a semantic one, with massive implications for those with least access to the gospel? Consider this 2009 data on the distribution of missionaries in proportion to world population. It's drawn largely from the World Christian Database and Joshua Project:[72]

> Let's not spend our mission money on what ministers primarily to ourselves.

Percentage of missionaries working among *reached* peoples (4 billion individuals): 90.4%

- Christians: served by 73.1% of missionaries
- Ethnic religious: served by 7.1% of missionaries
- Non-religious: served 3.4% of missionaries
- Muslims: served by 3% of missionaries
- Buddhists: served by 1.5% of missionaries
- Hindus: served by 1.3% of missionaries
- Others: served by 1% of missionaries

This leaves only 9.6%—less than 10%—of our missionaries working with the unreached (which this source's measurements list as 2.7 billion individuals):

- Unreached Hindus: served by 6% of missionaries
- Unreached ethnic religious (mostly animistic or tribal people): served by 3.8% of missionaries
- Unreached Muslims: served by 3% of missionaries
- Unreached non-religious people: served by .6% of missionaries

- Other unreached people: served by .2% of missionaries

The same source asserts that 99.5% of church spending is focused on the reached, while .5% is focused on the unreached.

If calling every Christian a missionary is supposed to elevate the spread of the gospel, why are proportionately few missionaries serving among peoples and places with few or no witnessing churches? Why is the Church expending the vast majority of her resources and energies where the gospel has already been preached and churches have been well established while those with little or no access to the gospel remain in spiritual darkness? Could it be that a mushy definition of missions makes our global task less clear, not more? Is it possible that when we combine local ministry and global missions into one category, we more often than not end up neglecting global missions?

## ETERNAL CONSEQUENCES

If every Christian is a missionary and reaching people with the same language and culture as our own is indeed missions, then crossing cultures to share the gospel would naturally be a low priority. In fact, if everything is missions, then the goal of the Great Commission might not be to make steady headway in reaching more nations, tribes, and tongues, but to win as many people to Jesus as possible. This may explain why the overwhelming majority of the Church's resources are spent at home and not on extending the gospel into new frontiers: If the Great Commission's goal is merely to win as many people to Christ as possible, then we should identify the places where the most spiritual new births are taking place and give it our all.

> If the Great Commission's goal is merely to win as many people to Christ as possible, then we should identify the places where the most spiritual new births are taking place and give it our all.

Let me take it one step further. If all ministry is equal and the goal is to win the highest number of souls possible, why should any church or missions agency pursue the unreached? After all, in most unreached peoples, gospel progress is painfully slow. That is precisely why they are unreached.

When every Christian is a missionary and everything is missions, the only difference between Orlando, Florida and Osh, Kyrgyzstan is geography, right? If we compare the populations we see that Orlando is much bigger, and probably has more lost people, right? Of course, in Orlando, there are hundreds of evangelical churches, countless ministries, and multiple Christian radio stations, while in Osh the presence of the gospel is so faint that most people couldn't hear about Jesus if they wanted to.

Here is where the eternal consequences come into focus: If churches don't make it a priority to reach all peoples and instead expend the vast majority of their energies and resources where the potential to reach the largest number of individuals with the gospel is possible, at home, then individuals within those people groups cut off from the light of the gospel can't hear it, at least not from us. When they perish in their sins without Christ, what awaits them is an eternity of conscious terrifying torment, separated from God.

Now anyone who loves Jesus, whether they think every Christian is a missionary or not, would say that's not right. We should be reaching the whole world. And I would say that the implication of the idea that we are all missionaries is one of the key reasons why so many churches in the West pay little or no attention to reaching all nations. After all, the work that they do at home is missions.

## A PICTURE OF HEAVEN

In Revelation 7:9-12, the curtains of time and space are peeled back and we are given a glimpse into the wonders of heaven:

"After this I looked, and behold, a great multitude that no one could number, from every nation, from all tribes and peoples and languages, standing before the throne and before the Lamb, clothed in white robes, with palm branches in their hands, and crying out with a loud voice, 'Salvation belongs to our God who sits on the throne, and to the Lamb!'

"And all the angels were standing around the throne and around the elders and the four living creatures, and they fell on their faces before the throne and worshiped God, saying, 'Amen! Blessing and glory and wisdom and thanksgiving and honor and power and might be to our God forever and ever! Amen.'"

Here we see the Lamb of God surrounded by the reward of His suffering, worshipers from the world over, from every nation, tribe, and tongue. This and this alone is the great end to which all of history is moving.

All of God's children will witness this endless celebration, but only those who were a part of the family business of making disciples of all nations will have the joy and honor of knowing that God in His mercy worked through them to bring these worshipers into His kingdom.

When every Christian is a missionary and every ministry is missions, I contend that we gut the mandate to reach all nations. That brings horrible, eternal consequences for individuals within people groups without access to the gospel who perish in their sins. In addition, God's children miss out on taking their part in the Great Commission. Let's not slow our efforts to reach the lost at home, but let's lift our eyes to the nations and increase our attention to those who have yet to hear about Christ.

So what's the big deal? Is it biblical to call every Christian a missionary, every work done in the name of Christ, a missions work? Does this lead to more missions work being accomplished or less? The answers to these questions matter. They matter in significant, serious, and eternal ways.

chapter 7

# WHAT NEXT?

by Denny Spitters and Matthew Ellison

## EMBRACING GOD'S GLOBAL PURPOSES

JOHN'S TEXT BEGAN, "Pastor Steve, about the meeting last night, as Executive and Missions Pastor, I'm greatly conflicted..."

It continued:

"I'm highly concerned with the many assumptions we are making about what missions and discipleship are and what they should be in our church. Without defining this more clearly, we seem to be wallowing in a no man's land of decision-making that lacks foundation and will effect what kind of church we will become. When could we discuss this?"

•••

When churches don't do missions well, it may be because they don't think about missions well. But what they believe the Bible teaches about missions and making disciples will be their cornerstone for vision, direction, and action. Biblical mission definitions can have a gigantic effect how local churches will make disciples of the nations—or if "the nations" emphasis of Jesus' command will even be acknowledged or embraced.

What are some of the barriers that might keep churches and their leaders from committing themselves to a Great-Commission-focused, intentional, international, disciple-making, church-planting paradigm of missions?

Although we have already addressed much of the unclear thinking and misunderstandings that exist today and how these effect the local church in missions, we would be remiss to ignore a primary and broadly embraced concept which some mission leaders describe as "sequentialism." This approach shows up in church belief and missions practice based upon Jesus' final words of Acts 1:8:

> "But you will receive power when the Holy Spirit has come upon you, and you will be my witnesses in Jerusalem and in all Judea and Samaria, and to the end of the earth."

The reading of these verses is often followed with the question, "Where is your Jerusalem, your Judea, your Samaria, and your ends of the earth?" I wonder if we have so over-individualized our approach to the Scriptures that we have obfuscated the main purpose of this text?

The idea of sequentialism is that Jesus was defining how the disciples were to advance the gospel by beginning with Jerusalem as their home town or base, then expanding to Judea and Samaria, and after that, going beyond to the end of the earth—in concentric circles. Think of the circles made by throwing a stone into a still pool of water.

Many who see missions in this light point out some important facts with which we agree:

- Jesus was decentralizing the gospel, moving it out from a Jewish-only context.
- God and His gospel are not ethnocentric; the gospel is for all peoples.
- God placed a dagger into the heart of racism—His Church will be multicultural.

- The gospel will have a "ripple effect" as Holy-Spirit-filled believers give witness to the gospel.

- Jesus is reinforcing his Matthew 28 emphasis on "all nations"—the gospel is for the whole world.

To interpret this passage as if Jesus is saying, "start at home with your neighbors, friends, and family as the primary focus and the center point for your witnessing," may seem quite rational. But is not true to the text. If such an approach was the Bible's teaching on this matter, we might need to replace the word *and* with *then*, as in, "You will be my witnesses in [your] Jerusalem, *then* in all [your] Judea and Samaria, and *then* to the end of the earth."

We often hear church leaders assuming such a model, however, saying, "Well, we are on mission right here in our back yard, our Jerusalem, and when we grow more disciples here and our church is bigger, we will go to our Judea and Samaria, and someday we will go to the end of the earth."

We confess we used to believe and embrace sequentialism with all of its pragmatic implications. It just made sense. Be faithful in small things and God will give us bigger ones, right? This also kept us in our comfort zone. But what happens to Jesus' command when we replace "and" with "then"?

Missiologist and church-planting catalyst David Garrison calls this "the deadly sin" or "heresy of sequentialism."[73] He implores us to read the passage as written, rather than a series of steps or stages. He describes sequentialism as separating into components what really ought to be embraced all at once.

"You shouldn't eat a cake, for example, one element at a time: flour, eggs, vanilla and then baking soda. The real enjoyment occurs when every element is present in every bite. Global missions is part of God's essential recipe for discipleship, not something you get to only in Christianity 401. It ought to be present in the first bite."[74]

When we grasp Garrison's point, we see that Jesus gave a simultaneous Jerusalem-to-the-ends-of-the-earth command which we see played out in the book of Acts and which provides a model for all disciples and churches. The vision of a ministry to all nations was to be part of all discipleship and church-planting efforts from the very beginning.

In addition, it may be helpful to observe that Jesus was not telling His disciples to start at home and to move on when they got that done. The disciples were Galileans. Jerusalem was not their home; it was a strategic launch point to the nations. In fact, after what happened to Jesus, the disciples may have seen Jerusalem as a hostile lion's den of opposition and death. Only when the Holy Spirit was given were they empowered to be witnesses among the nations gathered there and far beyond (Acts 2:4-11).

In *Gospel Meditation for Missions,* Pastor Chris Anderson points out that Pentecost was a day bursting with historical significance—the "birthday" of the New Testament Church. It was also a day filled with tremendous missionary significance. The Church born on Pentecost was unmistakably a multi-cultural and missionary Church.[75]

- Pentecost signified the mobility of the missionary Church. God's presence paralleled Moses' and Solomon's dedications of the Tabernacle and Temple as exemplified by the cloudy or fiery pillar now hovering as flames over individuals now comprising the Church of Jesus Christ. God's temple had been franchised and mobilized, prepared for the Great Commission. Rather than inviting the nations to "come!" to Jerusalem, the new temple—the Church—was commanded and enabled to "go!" to the nations.

- Pentecost signified the harvest of the missionary Church. Inaugurating His Church on a day of feasting and celebration was powerfully symbolic with a great spiritual harvest to come including more than 3,000 coming to Christ and baptized on that day.

- Pentecost signified the multi-ethnicity of the missionary Church. The international and multi-cultural nature of the Church is unmistakably foreshadowed in Acts 2 as evidenced by the diverse languages of various nationalities. Christianity was not culturally monolithic and wasn't Jewish, Hebrew, or Greek-centered. It was for all nations.

## A CASE OF MISSION DRIFT

What kind of disciples or churches will we become? How will we bring obedience and Great Commission priorities to our lives and churches?

Our direct observation is that the claim that "every ministry is missions" is directly linked to how the North American evangelical Church has been losing its moorings and its allegiance to the gospel. The gospel message, lifestyle, relevance, and pioneering apostolic core is disappearing from many of our churches. "Mission drift" has set in to the soul of our churches as we have left the essence and centrality of the gospel and replaced it with man-centered agendas.

We see this in the way many of our churches use our resources to eliminate our personal and corporate responsibility to sacrifice and identify with God's mission purposes, outsourcing missions to missionaries and national leaders in much the same way many congregations tend to do when they expect paid ministry staff to do the work of the church.

As mission efforts from outside the West have matured, some have said now is the time to "hand off the baton to the global Church of the South and get out of the way." Handing off the baton implies we are no longer in the race. While partnering and empowering others—especially empowering them to plant reproducing churches—wherever and whenever possible is an imperative, disconnecting ourselves from apostolic, cross-cultural, gospel-driven ministry violates our design and makes us ineffective and irrelevant even in our own context. The Bible has made it clear we are to persevere and occupy until He returns, as faithful servants and stewards of all He has given us. This is normal discipleship.

We believe that without a deep and well-developed commitment to the Great Commission which includes making disciples of all nations (not just serving in our own communities), our churches will die and the biblical gospel will be lost. When everything is missions, we dilute the fundamental, regular, daily expectations Jesus has for a normal lifestyle of discipleship.

We don't doubt the sincerity and passion of the many proponents of "everybody is a missionary" who want to stimulate evangelism and disciple making in their communities by living a gospel-centered missional lifestyle. We wholly believe they are fellow brothers and sisters in Christ who want His kingdom to advance.

We appeal to the Church, however, for renewed and reinvigorated commitment to the biblical, apostolic, missionary model and vision that fueled the apostle Paul, Barnabas, and Silas, and that has propelled the expansion of the Church through the last 2,000 years—that the gospel must reach those who have never heard (Romans 15:20). Paul said he had done this (Romans 15:19) from Jerusalem to Illyricum (Albania today). Rome was next on his list.

## GOING WHERE CHRIST IS NOT NAMED

Missionary David Hosaflook has some difficult words for us, passionately and prophetically stating,

> "Paul taught us that the essence of missions is going places where Christ is not already named (Romans 15:20). I don't understand why church planters so frequently ignore that

little word not. The mission is not to plant the coolest church in town, but the only church in town. Why target the Bible Belt when so many places don't even have a Bible? Roughly 35% of the world has no access to the Gospel. I'm not talking about the people in your neighborhood who have never heard 'a clear presentation of the Gospel' (but could if you would just cross the street). I'm talking about the 2.4 billion people who couldn't find a Christian if they tried. How is this possible? How many of our mission workers are even targeting them? I might be satisfied with a proportionate 35%. But get this: it's less than 5%. Tip a waitress 5% and she'll spit in your soup the next time you order lunch. Five measly percent is a yawn in the face of the Great Commissioner, a shrug at the plight of the damned. It's tantamount to telling the unreached to go to Hell." [76]

Strong language! But he goes on:

"Forgive my candor but I don't know how else to verbalize what our inaction is communicating. Our problem isn't fear—but a bigger issue. Christ is not our life (Philippians 1:21). We're self-absorbed. Distracted. Apathetic. Unimpressed at the stunning honor of fulfilling biblical prophecies. Passionate about anything other than the harvest fields of unreached souls—unreached not because they are unreachable, but because we have chosen not to reach them." [77]

Like us, you may react to this description of the Church today as overly dramatic, guilt-producing, or possibly quite harsh toward the Church. However, if we receive the observation as a well needed "poke" or "gut check," and move beyond our positive or negative emotional response, the challenge has significant merit. Have we become delinquent in taking up the honor of the Great Commission? After all, if there is something we want to get right, shouldn't it be the final words of our Lord's commission to us as His Church?

## FOUNDATIONAL STEPS TOWARD IMPLEMENTING OUR MISSION

If we choose intentionally to make disciples of all nations, what core steps should we take to start or make a new beginning? As His disciples, church leaders, and local church members, what action will we take to embrace an apostolic, disciple-making, church-planting paradigm that identifies and sends missionaries to the unengaged and unreached where no witness exists? What might it look like for our churches to become bold, intrepid, courageous churches like Antioch? We recommend the following foundational steps that will lead to healthy Great Commission practice and lifestyle.

### STEP I: REPENT, RECOVER, RECLAIM

A life of repentance is central and vital to living the gospel each day of our lives. Our hearts and minds need cleansing and renewal for our understanding of the Great Commission to be brought to its rightful place. To think about missions well, we must embrace the illuminating wisdom of God's Word as our guide, submitting other books and teachings to be held accountable to the missiological guidance of the Bible. If we place ourselves under its designs, standards, and principles, the Holy Spirit will lead and empower us to make the changes that will align us with His design for us as His local and global Church.

Has our wealth and comfort made us like the church in Laodicea (Revelation 3:15-18), neither hot nor cold and blind to our situation and how it could be changed? If this is so, we pray that God will help us repent, recover, and reclaim what we are losing, the stunning honor of being part of fulfilling biblical prophecies.

### STEP 2: WORSHIP, PRAY, FAST

Paul's first missionary journey was launched from a church given to worship, fasting, and prayer. The Holy Spirit spoke to them while they were consumed with these activities. We saw the same thing in Acts 1:13-14, preceding the giving of the Holy Spirit.

We often interact with churches and leaders who genuinely want to move into Great Commission action and are ready to talk tactics, asking, "What are the things we can do right now?" Jumping into action is very North American, woven into our culture with both good and bad results.

Yet the church in Antioch became a gospel slingshot because it was given to worship, prayer, and fasting, taking action only under the direction of the Holy Spirit. If we try to jump into things too fast, copying the models of other churches and expecting the same results, we leave out the direction and guidance of the Holy Spirit.

When churches ask us about their fresh ideas, we ask if their leadership has spent the time of worshipping, praying, fasting, and listening for God's voice and confirmation. So many of us are prone to take action without seeking God's divine direction. This usually leads to false starts.

What is the use of a great missions impulse if it's not from God's Spirit and embraced obediently by the Church?

"Missions is not the ultimate goal of the Church. Worship is. Missions exists because worship doesn't. Worship is ultimate, not missions, because God is ultimate, not man. When this age is over, and the countless millions of the redeemed fall on their faces before the throne of God, missions will be no more. It is a temporary necessity. But worship abides forever.

"Worship, therefore, is the fuel and goal of missions. It's the goal of missions because in missions we simply aim to bring the nations into the white hot enjoyment of God's glory. The goal of missions is the gladness of the peoples in the greatness of God. 'The Lord reigns; let the earth rejoice; let the many coastlands be glad!' (Psalm 97:1)."[78]

Oswald Chambers, defining the centrality of prayer and our dependency on Jesus, said, "Prayer does not fit us for the greater work; prayer is the greater work."[79]

We can we recover this foundation for our lives and churches simply by asking the Holy Spirit to guide us.

## STEP 3: EMBRACE PASSIONATE FIDELITY TO THE GOSPEL

The gospel is the reason missions makes sense. The gospel propels us forward in missions. We will soon wander off and lose our way in missions without a commitment of fidelity to the gospel as Paul defined in Romans 1:16-17,

> "For I am not ashamed of the gospel, for it is the power of God for salvation to everyone who believes, to the Jew first and also to the Greek. For in it the righteousness of God is revealed from faith for faith, as it is written, 'The righteous shall live by faith.'"

A valid missions paradigm must be anchored to the moorings of the true gospel, not turning "go therefore and make disciples of all nations" into anything and everything we can imagine it to be. Paul says in 1 Corinthians 15,

> "Now I would remind you, brothers, of the gospel I preached to you, which you received, in which you stand, and by which you are being saved, if you hold fast to the word I preached to you—unless you believed in vain."

Christ alone must be the center of missions message and motivation. How else can true transformation happen? Any other priority inserted above or on equal plane with this as our highest goal, whether it's a deep desire to "plant churches" or a noble quest to "bring freedom to those in sexual slavery," is a revision of the gospel that disempowers all efforts in missions. The goal of the gospel and the reason for its centrality is to make God renowned in every tribe, nation, language, and people.

## STEP 4: PURSUE A BIBLICAL DEFINITION FOR MISSIONS

If there is one pledge that we would delight to see churches and leaders make a commitment to, it would be in this area: to think deeply about missions, seeking out biblical direction and pursuing it.

We are sometimes amazed at how churches are deeply committed to accurate ecclesiology, soteriology, Christology, and many other matters of theology and doctrine, while neglecting missiology and its role in faith and practice; this leaves mission priorities and understanding up for grabs in our local churches. The ladder may be leaning against the wrong wall.

What we have discovered is that those who invest the time and effort it takes to walk the path of opening the Bible and letting it guide their thinking bring unity, understanding, guidance, and vision to their churches. As they align themselves with the Scriptures, their churches and their missions efforts are revitalized.

Some have sought and engaged outside coaching or consulting services for this process with positive results to help navigate these waters with church leaders. It takes effort and work. It's not easy but it is worth it.

Ultimately our missions definitions will determine the missions culture of our churches. Without this vital process, alignment and strategic missions vision will falter and fail. As the saying goes, "Culture eats strategy for breakfast." Because all roads do not lead to the same destination, an undefined missions definition will create a missions culture of "everything is missions" that will lead to confusion and unclear vision.

## STEP 5: DISCOVER YOUR ROLE IN THE GREAT COMMISSION

The Great Commission is a mandate for every disciple of Christ regardless of age or maturity, and every church regardless of size or global location. It is not optional. Every believer is to be living a lifestyle "on mission" for the purpose of its completion. Yet the distinction of roles is critical and depends on gifts, calling, and capability. How do we mobilize every believer for obedience to our Commander-in-Chief? The mobilizing of workers for the harvest incorporates many roles and no one is to be left out. We need trainers, encouragers, givers, organizers, elders, administrators, prayers, promoters, writers, senders, speakers, educators, and the list goes on, including apostolic missionaries.

We must overturn the tables of our missions thinking so that missionaries are no longer the professional stars on the playing field of missions whom we pay as our surrogates, while we observe as spectators from a distance, unengaged and uninvolved, cheering them on to victory as they move the gospel toward the end zone.

But it is no spectator sport. Everyone has a role in the Great Commission.

## STEP 6: MAKE DISCIPLES—OF ALL NATIONS

We love and fully support the aggressive emphasis some missional movements have embraced for proactive disciple making. Believers are charged to be on mission "to make disciples in their own back yard," their neighborhoods, workplaces, schools, etc. The goal of evangelism is to make disciples. Every believer is charged with the biblical mandate to make disciples who make disciples. We see this so strong in the life and teachings of Jesus. We also need our cross-cultural missionaries to be those who can disciple, wherever they may go. That's at the heart of the Great Commission.

> Simply blooming where we are planted and making disciples wherever we go is not the end of our commission.

Simply blooming where we are planted and making disciples wherever we go is not the end of our commission, however. David Mays pointed out that many of us tend to read Matthew

28:18-20 through the lens of what he calls "The Great Distortion."

"The object of 'disciple' is 'all nations.' Jesus did not say to disciple, or to disciple your family, or disciple whomever happens to be near, or disciple the people in your community, or disciple the people like you. He said to disciple ALL NATIONS, i.e. all peoples, all ethno-linguistic groups. 'Make disciples' cannot be divorced from 'all nations.' It is not fair, not legitimate, not biblical to claim the Great Commission for your church purpose and neglect the nations. It is to use the Scripture like a drunk uses a lamp post, for support rather than illumination."[80]

Is our commitment to disciple making anchored in the overall purpose of making disciples of all nations?

## STEP 7: CONSIDER THE VITAL ROLE OF A MOBILIZER

Mobilizers assemble or marshal people and supplies into readiness for service. A missions mobilizer is someone who understands the gravity and importance of what is at stake in the Great Commission and has embraced a vital role in the sending out of laborers. Ralph Winter describes the significance of these strategic motivators well:

"Here is a tragic fact: Only about one out of a hundred 'missionary decisions' results in actual career mission service. Why? Mainly because parents, friends, even pastors rarely encourage anyone to follow through on that kind of a decision. But what if that number could double to two out of a hundred? The effect would be explosive!"[81]

Mobilizers are those who "sound the alarm" to call the Church to the nations:

"Wouldn't it be more effective to go and wake 100 sleeping fireman to come and put out the blazing building than to just stand there alone throwing your buckets of water on it? These are the ones that yearn to be on the field, but have stayed behind to rally the troops. They form mission teams at their churches. They get people praying and giving and going. They organize short and long-term mission teams. They get books and materials into the Christian's hands."

Phil Parshall, missionary and author, described mobilizers this way:

"Someone must sound the rallying call. Those who desire to see others trained, prepared and released to ministry are known as mobilizers. Mobilizers stir other Christians to active concern for reaching the world. They coordinate efforts between senders, the local churches, sending agencies, and missionaries on the field. Mobilizers are essential. To understand the role of mobilizers, think of World War II as a parallel. Only 10% of the American population went to the war. Of those, only 1% were actually on the firing lines. However, for them to be successful in their mission, the entire country had to be mobilized!"[82]

Is God asking you to become a mission mobilizer? Some of us don't like war metaphors very much, but obeying Jesus' command to "disciple all nations" is essential to the future and survival of the North American Church. Mobilizers are that "war cry." We need the service and voice of thousands of "Chief Reminding Officers" who will encourage, marshal, and propel us into obedience of our Lord's last words.

## CONCLUSION

What is next for you? What idea do you need to consider and reflect upon? Is there a conversation you need to have?

If the observations and objections we have proposed in this book have caused agitation, let that move you to seek God for answers to your questions. It is our abiding desire and deep prayer that challenging the "every Christian is a missionary" and "every ministry is missions" concepts will motivate you to be like the noble Bereans who examined the Scriptures to see if the teachings of Paul and Silas were born of man or born of God (Acts 17:11). Let us not forget that we have a great cloud of witnesses cheering us on—anticipating our discovery of God's heart for every nation, tribe, and tongue. It is not too late for the North American Church to play a humble but still significant role in the Great Commission as we participate together in the Revelation 5:9 song:

"Worthy are you to take the scroll and to open its seals, for you were slain, and by your blood you ransomed people for God from every tribe and language and people and nation..."

# appendix a:
# THINKING DEEPLY

W E BELIEVE THAT POOR MISSIONS thinking leads to poor missions practices. We also believe that prayerful, deep, biblical thinking about missions leads to mission practices that please the One who commissioned us to make disciples of all the nations. Moreover, this blesses the world and blesses the Church.

"Knowing comes before doing and shapes doing" is a phrase we have used several times in the book which captures well the reason we felt it needed to be written. Our aim was to create tension in the hearts and minds of readers so that they could appraise whether their missions practices were being shaped by biblical truths and convictions or by assumptions, half-truths, and even myths. You may not agree with the positions we hold on these issues, but we hope and pray that you have been provoked or even irritated to the point that you will take time to consider God's position on "missions." His perspective is the one that matters.

Some who reviewed this book's original manuscripts suggested that we conclude with practical application points, and though there is nothing inherently wrong with that approach, we felt compelled that the thing to do is to think. Make no mistake, it is also time to "do," as so much of the world remains in spiritual darkness cut off from the light of Jesus. But for many of God's people, the "doing" would be far better done by better knowing the One who called us out of darkness into His marvelous light and knowing exactly what it was He called us to accomplish when we were commissioned into His global mandate.

So we end by exiting the very doors we walked through at the beginning of the book, asking the seven key questions again. How we answer them is not trivial—it matters in absolutely massive, significant, eternal ways. How will you respond?

## REFLECTION QUESTIONS

### 1. Do our definitions matter?

- Have you observed a cultural tendency to hesitate to assign objective meaning to words?

- What happens when we reserve the right to define biblical terms and theological concepts?

- What can happen when we and our churches come to common ground about key biblical concepts?

- Do you believe Jesus has left the interpretation and application of the Great Commission open to individual churches to decide or discover?

### 2. What is our mission?

- Do you believe God gave a clear mission to His Church? What is the mission that God gave His Church? Are the mission of God and the mission of the Church the same? Why or why not?

- How significant do you believe the Great Commission is in all that the Church is to do and be?

- If people in your church were asked, "what is missions?" what kind of responses would you hear? Do you think there would be widespread agreement or great variety in how they understand missions?

- What about church and mission leaders in your church? Do they share a common understanding of missions and the goals of your missions efforts?

- How might a narrow definition of missions or a narrow mission focus help or hinder your church in pursuing missions?

### 3. Why are we involved in missions?

- Consider the biblical claim that people must hear of and turn to Christ or face eternal damnation. If this is true, does it create missions urgency in your church?

- How might a robust mission vision benefit and bring life to your church?

- How does experiencing God's majesty, goodness, and mercy motivate and shape us for missions service?

- What other factors may motivate us for missions? Which ones are the most enduring or might have the most power to lead our churches into deeper Great Commission commitment?

### 4. Is every Christian a missionary?

- What is your church's perspective on this question? How does your leadership and congregation's understanding affect your missions ministry paradigm?

- What benefits might there be in calling every Christian a missionary? What harm might it cause?

- What are your convictions on this question? Do you believe every Christian is a missionary?

- How would you define what makes someone a missionary? What biblical passages support your conclusion?

### 5. How are missionaries sent?

- Do you think it makes sense to look to descriptions from the book of Acts for our mission models, or is it just written to tell us what happened in the early church?

- What roles can or should a church play in raising up and sending our workers? What are the responsibilities of the local church when it comes to confirming a call and equipping or caring for missionaries on the field?

- What are the dangers or pitfalls for missionaries who work as Lone Rangers, independent from a local church?
- What dangers or pitfalls might there be for churches who send out missionaries without national partners or sending agencies?

### 6. So what? What is at stake?

- Do you see the questions explored in this book as fundamental or more a matter of semantics?
- If you are a part of a congregation where everything is missions and every Christian is a missionary, what results do you see, positive or negative?
- This chapter explores several mission trends that the authors believe undermine a commitment to pursue the Great Commission. Which of these do you see in your church? Are there others?
- How do your mission definitions affect how your church allocates money, attention, and other resources?

### 7. What next? What might our next steps be?

- After reading this book and reflecting on these questions, who will you talk to? What is the most important conversation you need to have?
- What is the most important idea you need to consider or explore further?
- What is the most important decision you need to make or action you need to take?

# appendix b:
# RECOMMENDED RESOURCES

W E HAVE QUOTED and referenced numerous sources that explore the questions raised in this book. Would like to study these issues further? Below is a list of some of the resources we found most helpful.

## ARTICLES

Corwin, Gary. "MissionS: Why the "S" Is Still Important." *EMQ* 53:2 (April 2017), https://emqonline.com/node/3643.

DeYoung, Kevin. "The Goal of Missions and The Work of Missionaries." *The Gospel Coalition,* August 27, 2013, https://blogs.thegospelcoalition.org/kevindeyoung/2013/08/27/goal-missions-work-missionaries.

Ferdinando, Keith. "Mission: A Problem of Definition." *Themelios* 33:1 (2008), 46-59, http://s3.amazonaws.com/tgc-documents/journal-issues/33.1/Themelios_33.1.pdf.

Little, Christopher R. "The Case for Prioritism, Part 1." *Great Commission Research Journal* 7:2 (Winter 2016), 139-162, http://journals.biola.edu/gcr/volumes/7/issues/2/articles/139.

Long, Justin D. "Stop Trying to Persuade Everyone to Be a Missionary." *JustinLong.org,* https://justinlong.org/stop-persuading.php.

Mays, David. "The Great Distortion." *Davidmays.org,* http://www.davidmays.org/stories_distortion.html.

McKnight, Scot. "The Soul of Evangelicalism: What Will Become of Us?" *Patheos,* February 15, 2017, http://www.patheos.com/blogs/jesuscreed/2017/02/15/soul-evangelicalism-will-become-us.

Palpant Dilley, Andrea. "The World the Missionaries Made." *Christianity Today* 58:1 (January-February 2014), http://www.christianitytoday.com/ct/2014/january-february/world-missionaries-made.html.

Stetzer, Ed. "Involving All of God's People in All of God's Mission, Part 2." *Christianity Today* June 2010, http://www.christianitytoday.com/edstetzer/2010/june/involving-all-of-gods-people-in-all-of-gods-mission-part-2.html.

Traveling Team, The. "Goer, Sending Mobilizer, and Welcomer." *The Traveling Team,* http://www.thetravelingteam.org/articles/goer-sender-mobilizer-and-welcomer.

Wilton, Greg. "Are We All Missionaries? Redefining the Mission for All Believers." *Evangelical Missions Quarterly* 49:2 (April 2013), 134-135, https://www.emqonline.com/all_missionaries.

Winter, Ralph D. "The Two Structures of God's Redemptive Mission," *Perspectives on the World Christian Movement,* http://frontiermissionfellowship.org/uploads/documents/two-structures.pdf.

## VIDEOS

Piper, John. "Gospel Worship: Holy Ambition for All the Peoples to Praise Christ" (January 31, 2017, Bethlehem 2017 Conference for Pastor sand Church Leaders) *Desiring God,* http://www.desiringgod.org/messages/gospel-worship.

Sixteen:Fifteen, "1615 Rockpoint Church," *youtube.com,* (April 8, 2014), https://www.youtube.com/watch?v=de5m-4DobQsI.

## BOOKS AND BOOKLETS

Anderson, Chris, J.D. Crowley et al. *Gospel Meditations for Missions.* ChurchWorksMedia, 2011.

Beirn, Steve. *Well Sent: Reimagining the Church's Missionary Sending Process.* CLC Publications, 2015.

DeYoung, Kevin and Greg Gilbert. *What Is The Mission of The Church? Making Sense of Social Justice, Shalom, and the Great Commission.* Wheaton, IL: Crossway, 2011.

Greear, J.D. *Gaining by Losing: Why the Future Belongs to Churches that Send.* Grand Rapids, MI: Zondervan, 2015.

Horner, David. *When Missions Shapes the Mission: You and Your Church Can Reach the World.* Nashville, TN: B&H Publishing Group, 2011.

Lewis, Jeff. *God's Heart for the Nations.* Orlando, FL: BottomLine Media, 2015.

Mathis, David. *Finish the Mission: Bringing the Gospel to the Unreached and Unengaged.* Wheaton, IL: Crossway, 2012. (This book can be downloaded for free from http://www.desiringgod.org/books/finish-the-mission).

Newell, Marvin J. *Commissioned: What Jesus Wants You to Know as You Go.* Saint Charles, IL: ChurchSmart Resources, 2010.

Piper, John. *Let the Nations Be Glad: The Supremacy of God in Missions,* Third Edition. Grand Rapids, MI: Baker Academic, 2010.

## SIXTEEN:FIFTEEN: CHURCH MISSIONS COACHING

*1615.org*

Sixteen:Fifteen exists to help local churches discover and use their unique gifts in partnership with others to make Christ known among all nations. They help mobilize churches to become central players in the global mission of God, unleashing them to be His channel of blessing among the nations.

If you would like more information about how Sixteen:Fifteen can help unleash your church to reach the nations, please contact them at info@1615.org.

## THE MISSION TABLE: MOVING CONVERSATION THAT MOVES YOU TO ACTION

*missiontable.org*

The Mission Table is based on the belief that a critical step in effective, church-transforming, world-changing missions mobilization is to encourage thoughtful, transparent, and stimulating conversation. This web-based video episode resource tackles the critical and controversial topics impacting missions today.

The Mission Table is a resource of Sixteen:Fifteen.

## PIONEERS: CHURCH PLANTING AMONG THE UNREACHED

*pioneers.org*

For more than 35 years, Pioneers' passion has been to see God glorified among those who are physically and spiritually isolated from the gospel of Jesus Christ. Pioneers is an international movement that partners with local churches to mobilize teams to initiate church-planting movements among unreached people groups.

# ACKNOWLEDGEMENTS

THE NAMES OF ALL WHO INFLUENCE your thinking and assist you in a project of this nature can make a long list. I will keep it brief. To the more than 25 readers who gave critique and feedback on the original manuscript: thank you, brothers and sisters.

Unending thanks and love to my wife Nancy, who made this project happen with encouragement, critical thinking, and feedback.

Matthew, as my coauthor, I can't think of anyone I'd rather partner with to write a book. Thanks for your friendship and love for God's mission: "We didnah git dressed up fuh nuttin"!

Ted Esler, who has been such a helpful mentor in mission and, as a leader, has always asked the clarifying questions: May your tribe increase.

Marti Wade, thank you for making this book readable with patience wedded to an amazing skill set.

Much gratitude to Connie and Kelly, Greg, Mike, Charlie, Scott, Billy, Doug, Carey, Dona, and all current and past members of the Church Partnerships Team. Your dedication and passion for churches to engage in the Great Commission has propelled this forward.

Thanking an organization seems impersonal, but quality people demands an expression of deep appreciation. My thankfulness extends to everyone serving with Pioneers. You have sharpened and honed my life on mission: from our founders Ted and Peggy Fletcher, Steve Richardson who 12 years earlier offered an "opportunity knocking" moment, John Fletcher who gave me flexibility of workload while pointing to our preferred future of Acts 13 empowered churches, to Matt Green who after an early conversation about this project emailed me the completed cover art with a challenge: "All you need to do is fill in these covers": These pages are a reflection of all of you. I thank the Lord for the privilege of our partnership in the gospel.

*— Denny Spitters*

To Renee, my beautiful bride, and my wonderful children: Matthew, Caleigh, and Landin. Your presence in my life is tangible proof of God's amazing love for me. Every day that we spend together is a gift of mercy; I must be the richest, most blessed man on planet earth. Thank you for believing in me and for supporting me in our calling to make the nations glad in the glory of our great God and Savior Jesus Christ.

A special thank you to my mother Dorothy, who loved Jesus as much as anyone I have ever known and taught me repeatedly, as I knelt at my childhood bed, that "We love because He first loved us" (I John 4:19). "Mom, I will see you again, but not yet...not yet." I also want to thank Robertson McQuilkin, Virgil Dugan, Chris Abeyta, Saul Altamirano, Vic Jury, Dalton Jantzen, Gil Trusty, Denny Spitters, Tricia Morris, and the gracious and gifted team of people at Sixteen:Fifteen. Your friendship, encouragement, and influence have enlarged my heart for Jesus and expanded my vision for the worldwide spread of His glory. I can't wait until together in heaven, we experience the never-ending, ever-increasing joy of worshiping Jesus along with untold numbers of the redeemed from all nations, tribes, and tongues.

Finally, I must thank Dr. John Piper, whose books and teachings have been used by God to shepherd my heart and shape my understanding of world missions.

— *Matthew Ellison*

# ABOUT THE AUTHORS

**Denny Spitters,** Vice President of Church Partnerships for Pioneers USA, has served in many church staff roles as worship, missions, and small group pastor and understands the significance of missions in the local church. As missions pastor, he had multiple short-term and cross-cultural experiences. During his vocational ministry, Denny served on the staff of two mega-churches, directed a para-church ministry, and helped plant several churches. He also spent 15 years as a business owner.

**Matthew Ellison,** President and Church Missions Coach at Sixteen: Fifteen, served as a missions pastor at a mega-church for nine years, helping them transition from a reactive approach to world missions to proactive one. During this time he realized that there was a growing wave of churches no longer content to only support missions, instead they desired active global engagement. This led to the founding of Sixteen:Fifteen. Since 2004 he has been coaching churches across the United States, helping them to develop missions vision and strategy that fulfills the biblical mandate while taking into account their unique gifts, talents, and passions as local bodies of believers.

# NOTES

# ENDNOTES

1. Stephen Neill, *Creative Tension: The Duff Lectures,* 1958 (London: Edinburgh House Press, 1959), 81.

2. Christopher Wright, *The Mission of God's People: A Biblical Theology of the Church's Mission* (Grand Rapids, MI: Zondervan, 2010), 26.

3. Ed Stetzer, "Involving All of God's People in All of God's Mission, Part 2," *Christianity Today* (June 2010), http://www.christianitytoday.com/edstetzer/2010/june/involving-all-of-gods-people-in-all-of-gods-mission-part-2.html.

4. David J. Hesselgrave, foreword to *Commissioned: What Jesus Wants You to Know as You Go,* by Marvin J. Newell (Saint Charles, IL: ChurchSmart Resources, 2010), 12-13.

5. Ibid, 13.

6. Scot McKnight, "The Soul of Evangelicalism: What Will Become of Us?" *Patheos,* February 15, 2017, http://www.patheos.com/blogs/jesuscreed/2017/02/15/soul-evangelicalism-will-become-us.

7. Chris Anderson, J.D. Crowley et al, *Gospel Meditations for Missions* (ChurchWorksMedia, 2011), Day 1.

8. John Piper, *Let the Nations Be Glad: The Supremacy of God in Missions,* Third Edition (Grand Rapids, MI: Baker Academic, 2010), 35.

9. Eckhard J. Schnabel, *Paul the Missionary: Realities, Strategies, and Methods* (Downers Grove, IL: IVP Academic, 2008), 27-28.

10. Gary Corwin, "MissionS: Why the "S" Is Still Important," *EMQ* 53:2 (April 2017), https://emqonline.com/node/3643.

11. Ibid.

12. Marvin J. Newell, *Commissioned: What Jesus Wants You to Know as You Go* (Saint Charles, IL: ChurchSmart Resources, 2010), 23.

13. Ibid, 28.

14. Ibid, 25.

15. David Bosch, *Transforming Mission: Paradigm Shifts in Theology of Mission* (Maryknoll, NY: Orbis, 1991), 9.

16. Keith Ferdinando, "Mission: A Problem of Definition," *Themelios* 33:1 (2008), 48, http://s3.amazonaws.com/tgc-documents/journal-issues/33.1/Themelios_33.1.pdf.

17. Christopher Wright, *The Mission of God: Unlocking the Bible's Grand Narrative* (Downers Grove, IVP Academic, 2006), 23.

18. Ibid, 47.

19. Ibid, 22.

20. Ibid, 61.

21. Ibid, 25-26.

22. Ibid, 416.

23. Ferdinando, "Mission: A Problem of Definition," 55.

24. Christopher R. Little, "The Case for Prioritism, Part 1," *Great Commission Research Journal* 7:2 (Winter 2016), 140, http://journals.biola.edu/gcr/volumes/7/issues/2/articles/139.

25. Ibid, 148

26. Ibid, 141

27. Ibid.

28. Jeff Lewis, personal email correspondence with Denny Spitters, April 19, 2015.

29. Piper, *Let the Nations Be Glad,* 137.

30. *JoshuaProject.net* estimates that in 2017, 6,733, or 40.6%, of the world's 16,584 people groups are unreached. They define a people group as the largest group within which the gospel can spread as a church-planting movement without encountering significant barriers of understanding or acceptance, though this is measured almost exclusively in term of language and ethnicity. Unreached groups are those that lack enough followers of Christ and resources to evangelize their own people.

31. Todd M. Johnson and Gina A. Zurlo, eds, "World Christian Database," *gordonconwell.edu,* http://www.gordonconwell.edu/ockenga/research/documents/Statusof-GlobalChristianity2017.pdf.

32. Ibid. The authors report personal income of all Christians at $53,000 billion ($53 trillion), and income of global foreign missions as $53 billion.

33. David Penman, "How Can They Hear?" Lausanne II: Second International Congress on World Evangelization (Manila, Philippines, 1989), https://www.lausanne.org/wp-content/uploads/2007/06/255.pdf.

34. Sixteen Fifteen, "1615 Rockpoint Church," *youtube.com,* (April 8, 2014), https://www.youtube.com/watch?v=de5m4DobQsI.

35. J.D. Greear, *Gaining by Losing: Why the Future Belongs to Churches that Send* (Grand Rapids, MI: Zondervan, 2015).

36. A.W. Tozer, *Men Who Met God: Twelve Life-Changing Encounters* (Camp Hill, PA: Christian Publications, 1986), 12.

37. A.W. Tozer, *Whatever Happened to Worship?* (Camp Hill, PA: WingSpread Publishers, 2006), 70.

38. Piper, *Let the Nations Be Glad*, 35.

39. Tozer, *Met Who Met God,* 17.

40. John Piper, "At the Price of Christ's Own Blood," *Desiring God,* May 7, 1989 (sermon), http://www.desiringgod.org/messages/at-the-price-of-gods-own-blood.

41. Charles H. Spurgeon, "A Sermon and a Reminiscence," *Sword and the Trowel* (March 1873), http://www.spurgeon.org/s_and_t/srmn1873.php.

42. Winkie Pratney, "Winkie Pratney Quotes," o*Christian.com,* http://christian-quotes.ochristian.com/Winkie-Pratney-Quotes.

43. Nikolaus Ludwig von Zinzendorf, "Quotes by Count Zinzendorf," *sermonindex.net,* http://

www.sermonindex.net/modules/articles/index.
php?view=article&aid=32366.

44. Alan Hirsch and Lance Ford, *Right Here Right Now: Everyday Mission for Everyday People* (Grand Rapids, MI: Baker Books, 2011), 63.

45. Justin D. Long, "Stop Trying to Persuade Everyone to Be a Missionary," *JustinLong.org,* https://justinlong.org/stop-persuading.php.

46. Kevin DeYoung, "The Goal of Missions and The Work of Missionaries," *The Gospel Coalition,* August 27, 2013, https://blogs.thegospelcoalition.org/kevindeyoung/2013/08/27/goal-missions-work-missionaries.

47. Herbert Kane, *The Making of a Missionary,* Second Edition (Grand Rapids, MI: Baker Book House, 1987), 14.

48. Os Guiness. *The Call: Finding and Fulfilling the Central Purpose of Your Life* (Nashville, TN: Word, 1998), 47.

49. Brian McLaren, *A Generous Orthodoxy* (Grand Rapids, MI: Baker Book House, 2004), 119.

50. Craig Ott and Stephen J. Strauss. *Encountering Theology of Mission: Biblical Foundations, Historical Developments, and Contemporary Issues* (Grand Rapids, MI: Baker Academic, 2010), 225.

51. Greg Wilton, "Are We All Missionaries? Redefining the Mission for All Believers," *Evangelical Missions Quarterly* 49:2 (April 2013), 134-135, https://www.emqonline.com/all_missionaries.

52. Ibid.

53. Andrea Palpant Dilley, "The World the Missionaries Made," *Christianity Today* 58:1 (January-February

2014), 40, http://www.christianitytoday.com/ct/2014/january-february/world-missionaries-made.html.

54. Ibid.

55. Robert Royal, "The Missionary Position," *The Catholic Thing* (June 25, 2014), https://www.thecatholicthing.org/2014/06/25/the-missionary-position.

56. Robert J. Priest et al, "Researching the Short-Term Missions Movement," *Missiology* 34:4 (October 2006), 431-450, http://journals.sagepub.com/doi/abs/10.1177/009182960603400403.

57. "The Beginning," *Travel the Road,* https://www.traveltheroad.com/the-beginning.

58. Kevin DeYoung and Greg Gilbert, *What Is The Mission of The Church? Making Sense of Social Justice, Shalom, and the Great Commission* (Wheaton, IL: Crossway, 2011), 241.

59. Steve Beirn, Well Sent: *Reimagining the Church's Missionary Sending Process* (Washington, PA: CLC Publications, 2015), 97.

60. David L. Frazier, *Mission Smart* (Memphis, TN: Equipping Servants International, 2014), 5.

61. Ibid, 9-10.

62. George W. Peters, *A Biblical Theology of Missions* (Chicago, IL: Moody Press, 1984), 214.

63. Beirn, Well Sent, 109.

64. "Episode 1," *The Mission Table,* http://missiontable.org/project/episode-1-everyone-is-a-missionary.

65. Sarah Eekhoff Zylstra, "Lawsuit Claims Gospel for Asia Misused Most Donations to 10/40 Window," *Christianity Today* (February 12, 2016), http://www.christianitytoday.com/news/2016/february/lawsuit-gospel-for-asia-misused-donations-gfa-kp-yohannan.html.

66. K.P Yonnanan, *Revolution in World Missions: One Man's Journey to Change a Generation* (Carrollton, TX: GFA Books, 2004), 158, 217.

67. Bob Finley, *Reformation in Foreign Missions* (Xulon Press, 2005), 10. See also http://www.christianaid.org/AboutUs/ReformationInForeignMissions.aspx and a public discussion of Finley's points carried out in the pages of *Mission Frontiers* magazine, e.g., http://www.missionfrontiers.org/issue/article/what-is-the-story.

68. David Mathis, *Finish the Mission: Bringing the Gospel to the Unreached and Unengaged* (Wheaton, IL: Crossway, 2012), 22-23, http://www.desiringgod.org/books/finish-the-mission.

69. Brandy Zadrozny, "Lawsuit: Controversial Pastor Ran Mars Hill Megachurch Like a Crime Syndicate," *The Daily Beast,* February 29, 2016, http://www.thedailybeast.com/articles/2016/02/29/lawsuit-controversial-pastor-ran-mars-hill-megachuch-like-a-crime-syndicate.html.

70. Ibid.

71. Ibid.

72. Ralph D. Winter and Bruce A. Koch, "Finishing the Task," *Perspectives on the World Christian Movement* (Pasadena, CA: William Carey Library, 2009), 545.

73. David Garrison, *Church Planting Movements: How God Is Redeeming a Lost World,* sixth printing edition (Midlothian, VA: WIGTake Resources, 2004), 243-245.

74. *David Garrison's thoughts summarized in Greear's Gaining by Losing,* 153.

75. Chris Anderson, "Pentecost and Missions," in *Gospel Meditations for Missions,* Day 16.

76. David Hosaflook, "Yonder Village," in G*ospel Meditations for Missions,* Day 31.

77. Ibid.

78. Piper, *Let the Nations Be Glad,* 35.

79. Oswald Chambers, "The Key of the Greater Work," *My Utmost for His Highest,* https://utmost.org/the-key-of-the-greater-work.

80. David Mays, "The Great Distortion," *davidmays.org,* http://www.davidmays.org/stories_distortion.html.

81. "Every World Christian a Mobilizer," *The Traveling Team,* http://www.thetravelingteam.org/articles/every-world-christian-a-mobilizer.

82. "Goer, Sending Mobilizer, and Welcomer," *The Traveling Team,* http://www.thetravelingteam.org/articles/goer-sender-mobilizer-and-welcomer.